$...making it
and
keeping it !

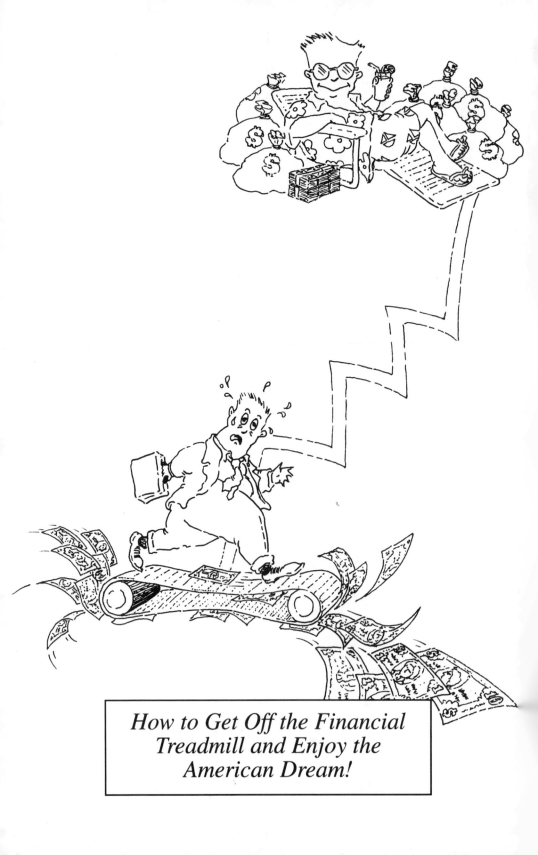

How to Get Off the Financial Treadmill and Enjoy the American Dream!

$...making it
and
keeping it !

The Common Sense Guide
to Financial Wellbeing

Alexander Odishelidze

There are no references in this book to specific sources of statistical information. The reason is that any such "facts" I present here are not material to the real focus of the book. What is important is whether the reader comes away from reading this book positively impacted by its general content.

However, I do wish to acknowledge that all the quotations contained here have been picked from "Economic and Business Quotations" by Michael Jackman, published by Macmillan & Co.

Publisher:

Employee Benefits Associates, Inc.
Publishing Division
#33 Bolivia Street, Fourth Floor
Hato Rey, Puerto Rico 00917
(809) 763-5345

ISBN (clothbound edition) 0-9633405-0-6
ISBN (paperback edition) 0-9633405-1-4

This book is dedicated to "Standup Harlem" which exemplifies the spirit of people picking themselves up by their bootstraps; making a real life for themselves, in spite of their HIV condition, rather than succumbing to the streets.

A portion of the proceeds of this book will be donated to "Standup Harlem" and other similar organizations that are an example of individuals taking charge of their own lives.

Contents

Men do not desire to be rich, but to be richer than other men.

JOHN STUART MILL, 1848

You are affluent when you buy what you want, do what you wish and don't give a thought to what it costs.

J. PIERPONT MORGAN, 1897

America is not a land of money, but of wealth - not a land of rich people, but successful workers.

HENRY FORD, 1935

I have been rich and I've been poor.
Believe me, honey, rich is better.

SOPHIE TUCKER, 1945

Preface

THIS BOOK IS DESIGNED TO HELP YOU GET RICH.

By "rich," I mean to reach a point where within the next five to ten years, and well before the time you plan to retire, you will have enough capital to maintain your standard of living without having to worry about earning an income.

Being rich may have little to do with how much money you have. Many people have a high net worth and high incomes, but still have to worry about earning that income so they can pay their bills.

This book is not for everyone.

If you already have a few million dollars in the bank and are working not because you need the income but to pile more millions on top of the ones you already have, or if you are broke and couldn't care less about being financially independent, you should return this book and get your money back.

On the other hand, if you lost your job or business and the capital that you now have won't pay your bills for more than a year or two, then this book is for you, regardless of whether your income is $30,000 or $300,000 a year.

Especially if you are like most Americans, earning a respectable middle class living, yet your bills are choking you and you see no end in sight to this financial treadmill, watching tens, perhaps hundreds of thousands of dollars pass through your hands each year - then this book could transform your life.

This book contains the distillation of my own experience and how "I did it" by the time I was in my mid-forties. It took me less than ten years once I learned "The Process." But it took me twenty years before that to learn "The Process." If I had read this book when I was first starting out in life, I might have saved myself those twenty years of hard work, frustrations, disappointments and dead ends.

This book does not fall into the category of "Do as I say but not as I do," which is where most books written on personal finance belong. Most of those authors are still struggling to "make it" while they try to tell you how it is done.

You will find no hypothetical theories here.

I "did it" and I want to share with you my experience.

And "I did it" quietly without earning huge amounts of money by patenting some brilliant invention, or starting some extremely successful business, or by being a whiz on Wall Street or in Real Estate.

This book is not about "methods" (even though I do discuss some methods in detail). Effective methods are a dime a dozen and they are useless unless the right attitudes are there to drive them.

However, after reading this book, with your attitudes firmly in place, if you want a really good book on methods, pick up Jonathan Pond's "The New Century Family Money Book" published by Dell. You'll have more than enough nitty gritty to sink your teeth into.

One thing you won't find in this book is THE way to become rich. This is because I don't believe there is any one way to do it. The only right way is your way.

This book IS about attitudes and values. And if you plug into the "attitudes and values" that I describe in this book, you will find your way of "making it and keeping it."

My purpose is to help you reexamine your own attitudes and values by sharing with you stories, sayings, personal experiences, proverbs, quotations and explanations that I hope will cause you to think and develop an effective game plan that is uniquely yours.

And sometimes, to drive my point home, and especially to help you embrace this viewpoint, I may use a lot of repetition.

This book is not sophisticated. It is definitely simplistic. Making money and keeping it is the crudest thing one can do.

People who are not rich erroneously believe that it takes brilliance, dedication to hard work, sacrifice and a unique and complicated method to become rich. They are always looking for sophistication and complexity. That's why they are not rich.

Getting rich is simple, easy and boring. (Staying rich however, is not as simple and easy because you are constantly beating off armies of people who want to take it away from you, and who may be a lot smarter than you are.) But once you get there, being rich helps you have fun, frees you from worry and exposes you to a fulfilling, rewarding and exciting life.

For the most part, there are no new revelations in this book. Most of the things you will read here, you probably have read or heard somewhere before.

A couple of new ideas you will pick up here deal with two simple formulas for tracking your progress of wealth accumulation that I personally have developed. Given my lack of formal education in mathematics, they are very simple indeed.

Those are "The Wealth Factor" and the "Financial Independence Factor"(chapter #9).

In addition, I use my 20 years of experience in the securities and insurance business to share with you some inside information about how insurance companies and brokerage houses operate with their schemes to "get your money."

This type of information is jealously guarded by many companies and is not available to the consumer public. They will go to great lengths to conceal how they really formulate their sales strategies. However, if you understand how financial institutions think, it will help you hang on to your hard earned dollars when they come knocking on your door.

So why should you read this book?

To begin with, this book will help you create the attitudes and values you need to get rich, which, as I said before, are far more important than any specific method you might read about.

Secondly, if you still have to work to pay your bills, you must not yet have grasped your personal formula for getting rich. This book will give you the insight that will help you "put it all together." It will help you get off the financial merrygoround that most of us are on, and position you to reach your financial independence goals.

An editor who reviewed this book suggested that people don't want to change their attitudes and values that might have been part of their psyche for many years.

She said: "If you want to sell a lot of copies of your book, you should not attempt to create change. It will rub your readers the wrong way! Just tell the people what they want to hear and make them feel good".

That's not why I went through this exercise.

From my viewpoint, this book would not be successful if it sold a million copies yet not one person became better off from reading it.

But it will be a success if just a few of you who do read it, are able to enjoy some positive change in your life.

The degree of wealth you may achieve, after reading this book, is strictly in your hands. My intention is that in reading this book you become much more effective at handling your personal finances and as an end result enjoy your life a whole lot better.

And that alone may be worth the price of this book and the time it takes you to read it.

Acknowledgments

There are a few people without whom this book may never have become a reality. I would like to acknowledge their influence on my life and on this work.

My two sons, Sasha and Michael, who brought love and special meaning to my life. My first wife, Julie, without whom there would not have been a story to tell. Inez, who encouraged me to do it. Jane, who guided me through the countless rewrites, and gave me insights to help me define what I really wanted to say. And Aixa, who made it all come out on paper.

The desire of bettering our condition comes with us from the womb and never leaves us until we go to the grave.

ADAM SMITH, 1776

You can only drink thirty or forty glasses of beer a day, no matter how rich you are.

ALDOLPHUS A. BUSCH, 1924

We can do without any article of luxury we have never had; but when once obtained, it is not human nature to surrender it voluntarily.

THOMAS C. HALIBURTON, 1836

Inequality of property will exist as long as liberty exists.

ALEXANDER HAMILTON, 1788

Penny wise and pound foolish.

WILLIAM CAMDEN, 1605

CHAPTER 1

If you want to get rich, don't "major in minors"!

THERE HAVE BEEN MANY BOOKS WRITTEN on personal finance, some of them good and some of them not so good. I have not read all of them but I have read enough of them to realize that most of these books deal with the technical aspects of reducing taxes, investment strategies; personal budgeting and saving, taking advantage of loopholes in tax and other laws, smart shopping to save money and other themes that strictly deal with the question of "how to" in handling specific subjects related to personal finances.

These books focus on helping someone get more efficient at managing their money rather than helping them become more effective with their dollars. They talk about doing things right instead of doing the right things.

And that, in essence, is, in my opinion, the real problem with most personal finance books. They emphasize "efficiency" instead of "effectiveness." They show you how to "major in minors"!

Think of it this way, if all it takes is efficiency with money to make a fortune, all accountants would be rich.

All the methods to maximize your dollars are totally useless unless you are going to use them. Unless your attitude is "right," all these methods will eventually wind up on the back burner of your brain, filed away for some future reference. You promise yourself you will use them tomorrow, next week or maybe the next year.

1

Before you begin any kind of a plan to put your financial house in order, you need to understand why you are doing it. You need a strong reason or motive. And you also need to visualize very clearly the end result that you would like to achieve.

Just making more money on your investments or increasing your net worth is not enough. You need a real reason that is very much a personal and emotional reason why you should develop the disciplines needed to take charge of your financial future.

If you don't have this basic motive, you will probably get tripped up by your ego and/or your greed and in the end wind up broke, regardless of how sophisticated your plan might have been.

For ten years now, I have been in the business of advising people on their personal finances. In the beginning, when I first began working with clients and developing their "Financial Plans," I tried applying the information I learned in courses such as the Certified Financial Planner and the Chartered Financial Consultant programs. I became a C.F.P. and a Ch.F.C. and honestly believed that these designations would make me qualified to effectively guide my clients in reaching their financial objectives.

These courses were loaded with technical information about taxes, investments, insurance, estate planning, etc., and I genuinely thought that I was doing my clients a service by drowning them with reams of computer printouts that included a lot of the above mentioned technical nonsense.

After a while I began to realize what I learned in all those courses had nothing to do with personal finance. It had a lot to do with taxes, investments, etc., yet it had very little to do with why and how some people are truly able to attain personal freedom and financial independence and while others, no matter how rich they may appear to the world outside, are, in fact, prisoners of the financial web they managed to spin for themselves, a web that keeps them chained to their desks 52 weeks a year.

By that time I was in my mid-forties, and I began thinking about my own life and where it had led me.

But most of all, I began thinking about why I was where I was and my clients weren't.

By that time I worked about six months a year, spending the rest of the time skiing at my house in Vail, Colorado, or traveling around the world discovering exotic people and places.

Even though I was still actively earning a living, I knew if my income had stopped, it really wouldn't have mattered because I could continue to live my lifestyle without earning another dime, probably for the rest of my life.

What was amazing to me about my personal situation was that even though over the years I had accumulated a seven-figure net worth, I had personally never earned over $100,000 per year.

Yet my clients, most with incomes and net worths much higher than mine, were stuck with their noses to the grindstone, barely managing to squeeze two or three weeks vacation every year. Was it luck? Or was it something else?

As I reflect back to answer that question, I certainly don't think that I was blessed with an extraordinary amount of good fortune. I didn't inherit any money nor did I possess a brilliant mind capable of grasping the most intricate problems. The truth is that I never got past the tenth grade and finally got a high school equivalency diploma in the U.S. Army.

My life was certainly not a straight shot to the top. As a matter of fact it has been a financial roller coaster, including a business failure, a couple of divorces, paying child support and alimony, getting fired from my job a couple of times, moving to and from about five different sections of the country - not to mention having done time as a single parent and putting a couple of kids through college.

All of the above are not exactly conducive to accumulating a high net worth, let alone becoming independent of earned income.

Yet there I was, enjoying freedom and financial independence at a relatively young age, where under most circumstances I should have been broke.

What happened?

That's when I decided that everything I had read on personal finance, and all the courses I had taken on "Financial Planning," along with my designations such as C.F.P. and Ch.F.C., were nothing more than a bunch of totally useless information that had no relationship to achieving personal finance goals and especially, attaining financial independence.

What finally convinced me of this was taking a close look at my colleagues, who were in the same profession, giving speeches all over the country and writing books and articles on how to get rich, yet were broke themselves.

What right did they have to offer advice on investments, wealth accumulation, estate planning, etc., while they were two months behind on their mortgage payment?

That's when I knew the real answer was not in the textbooks which were loaded with many minor details about personal finance, but instead in our own attitudes and how strongly we had developed our personal, internal value system.

Perhaps in that department I was truly "lucky." In my early years I had the opportunity to develop some definite attitudes and personal values that, as I think back, have helped guide me to where I could sit down and write this book.

Probably the most important thing that I learned was the real meaning of a certain four letter word: "need."

I don't mean to bore you with a lot of details about my life, but in order for me to make the point, I need to quickly give you some background.

Being born and raised under the Communist system, as I was, gives one a different perspective on life and probably positions one very well to function successfully as a capitalist.

The main reason being that once you get to a country that operates on the free enterprise system, you are like a kid in a candy store.

You see opportunities that most people who have spent their whole lives living there never get a glimpse of, and all you have to do is reach out and take them.

Can you imagine how great it feels not to worry about going to jail if you make money in business?

"Vat a contry!" as a fellow immigrant, Yakov Smirnoff used to say.

Since I was a Russian (Georgian actually) living in Yugoslavia, Tito kicked my family out of the country when he split with the Soviet Union.

I was eleven at the time and wound up spending two years in Displaced Persons camps, first in Italy and then in Germany. For those who are not familiar with a DP camp, let me paint you a picture.

Hundreds of people jammed into huge tents. Mud floors. People sleeping in double bunks, hanging blankets for privacy from the top bunk to the bottom bunk. Cold winter wind blowing in from the side of the tent. Outside, troughs with running cold water for washing and shaving. Outside latrines. It's freezing out there. A cup of hot water for breakfast. A bowl of dried spaghetti for lunch and dinner. No medical facilities. People coughing all night. Tuberculosis rampant. In the morning, the dead bodies are carried out in stretchers.

As soon as you get into a DP camp you apply for a country to admit you. Canada, Australia, New Zealand, Argentina, Venezuela, just to name a few, were some of the countries accepting immigrants. The name of the game was to survive long enough in the camp without catching TB until a country accepted you. Once you got TB, however, you were stuck in the camp until you died.

It's a race against time. To get accepted before you got sick. This was a real race. Life or death, right down to the wire.

So you had to hustle to survive. Get nutrition so that you didn't catch TB.

I figured out a gimmick. I noticed that the guards ears got cold under their helmets. I learned to knit and invented an ear muff that fit nicely under the helmet band. I scrounged for old sweaters and converted them to ear muffs and traded those for chocolates, milk and other survival goods.

In the summer, I would sneak out of the camp and go down where the cruise ships docked. There I dove for pennies that the passengers threw overboard just to see the little ragamuffins scramble and almost drown for them. It worked. I'm here!

I finally got accepted by Canada before I could catch TB and was soon on a ship headed for the new world and the land of opportunity.

As soon as we landed, we were placed in other camps. But this time it was different. We had plenty of food, the barracks were warm, and we even had medical care. This was living!

But here is the real point of this story. Local volunteers would come to the camps and take the kids and teenagers into their homes in order to get them acclimated to the New World.

I will never forget my first trip to the supermarket. Can you imagine, after two years in a DP camp, being exposed to all this food? It was awesome!

Anyway, as the lady who took us around the supermarket was doing her shopping, she would pick up an item and say, "We need this," and "We need that." Not speaking any English, I was curious what the word "need" meant. I somehow communicated this to her and she somehow explained it to me. It was probably pure osmosis but I got the picture. And that was where I became totally confused.

From my frame of reference one did not "need' strawberry jam. One needed bread because when one got hungry, bread filled the stomach.

But strawberry jam? Totally superfluous and unnecessary!

This was my first lesson in values, and especially in what "need" really meant. It was the basis upon which I built my attitude toward material posessions.

Since then, whatever problems I might have encountered in my life really didn't matter because anything outside a DP camp was pure gravy.

Now don't get me wrong. I am not suggesting that in order for you to become financially independent you need to spend a couple of years in a DP camp.

But what I am saying is if you really take a close look at what it is you need in this life to be happy, you will find that you are probably wasting a lot of your dollars and energies on frills that mostly go into impressing your neighbors and feeding your ego.

I am also not saying that if a Mercedes will make you happy, you shouldn't have one. Even I have owned a few of those! What I am saying is that before you buy that Mercedes, make sure it is the income on your capital that is buying it and not your earned income.

And that, in a nutshell, is what this book is all about.

There are forces out there that keep you from accumulating capital or if you have accumulated it, prevent you from keeping it.

Many of those forces are internal, attitudinal; some of them are external and may be beyond your control. You need to recognize what they are and learn how to deal with them.

If you don't you will probably earn a lot of money in your lifetime but will work too hard, enjoy life too little, and in the end wind up unhappy and broke.

Throughout this book I attempt to identify those forces, and offer approaches to dealing with them effectively.

The solutions are simple, common sense solutions that anyone can apply and cost little or nothing.

As I said in the beginning, this book is not intended to offer a specific blueprint, or a step by step method of winning the money game. The real purpose of the book is to help you form the attitudes needed to win this game and to re-examine your personal values so that you can fine tune them in order to position yourself to make your own personal finance decisions, and not react to a set of conditioned responses for which you have been programmed in the past.

Twenty five years ago I picked up a book whose title claimed it to be a step-by-step method of becoming a millionaire in Real Estate. The first paragraph of the first chapter jumped right into this method. It said: "First you take a million dollars and buy a good commercial office building." If I had a million dollars then, I probably would not have bought that book. So that was as far as I got before I threw the book away.

It's the same with most personal finance books. They assume you have either lot's of income available after expenses for savings and/or plenty of money already saved in the bank.

Unfortunately, most of us spend what we earn regardless of how much we earn.

As a nation (and perhaps much of today's world) we have come down with a terrible sickness. This sickness manifests itself in a material consumption frenzy. As a result, we are in debt as individuals, and are in debt as a nation. We are totally addicted to our spending habits and our addiction is fueled and encouraged not only by the advertising media but by our government.

Have you noticed how much attention our economists put on measuring the "consumer confidence index" which really drives our economy. We readily admit that we are a "consumer economy" and our national prosperity and recessions are dictated by how much or how little, we, the consumers, spend.

We can predict how good next year will be by how good a Christmas season our department stores may have had.

We spend ourselves into oblivion because we almost feel it is the patriotic thing to do. It is the American way - and also the way straight to the poorhouse.

The only way we can get off this treadmill is by going through an internal metamorphosis that will change the way we feel about money and material possessions. We have to let go of the premise that our value as individual human beings is somehow measured in the dollars and cents value of the toys that we accumulate and hold up for the whole world to see. We have to learn how to measure our personal net worth not in relation to someone else's wealth, but strictly in terms of the meaning it may have to us.

Once we come in touch with our real needs and wants, we will be amazed by how much money there really is left over after every paycheck and how quickly we begin to accumulate real capital.

Our shift in our inner values and attitudes will manifest itself in a corresponding increase in our bank accounts. It is a remarkable process which happens with very little effort.

And if I did it so can you!

Man today is fascinated by the possibility of buying more, better and especially new things. He is consumption-hungry. The act of buying and consuming has become a compulsive, irrational aim, because it is an end in itself, with little relation to the use or pleasure in the things bought and consumed.

ERICH FROMM, 1965

Truly it is a reproach to a man that he knows not when he hath enough; when to leave off; when to be satisfied.

WILLIAM PENN, 1668

With the great part of rich people, the chief employment of riches consists in the parade of riches.

ADAM SMITH, 1776

It is the superfluous things for which men sweat.

SENECA, c. A.D. 63

Remember that there is nothing stable in human affairs; therefore avoid undue elation in prosperity, or undue depression in adversity.

SOCRATES, c. 399 B.C.

CHAPTER 2

Income is not wealth, but our egos won't allow us to believe it!

OVER THE LAST 50 YEARS our national attitudes have done a full 360 degree turn.

During the 40's, 50's and 60's, the Great Depression kept our minds constantly focused on the possibility that there might be another economic upheaval, as a result of which we could once again wind up without a roof over our head. So we were frugal, we saved for a rainy day and we kept our money in our pockets.

The prosperity we enjoyed during this period and through the 70's and especially the 80's, on the other hand, gave a false feeling that this bonanza will continue forever, so that there became no need to worry about taking care of tomorrow.

Those were the attitudes of the 20's. The days when business was king, the banks were considered "safe" and the stockmarket had no ceiling. Sound familiar?

A couple of years ago, an economist by the name of Dr. Ravi Bhatra, came out with a theory that the 90's will witness one of the greatest world depressions we have ever seen.

Part of this theory was based on the fact that a Russian economist named Kondratieff, who studied economic swings over the centuries, concluded that the world experiences a major depression every 60 years or so. This theory was accepted worldwide as the "Kondratieff wave".

When the book came out, even though it was a best seller, as a

11

theory it was by and large poo-poohed by most economists.

Are we really due for another "Great Depression"?

I have no idea. However, I do know that history has shown us cycles of recession, depression and, not to forget, "Good Times." But how do we really define a "depression"? I've heard the difference between a depression and a recession described in the following way: "Recession is when your neighbor is out of work, and a depression is when you are out of work."

Today, the signs of bad times are all around us. All we need to do is take a walk down any downtown street in any major city and we will see the armies of homeless rummaging through the trash, panhandling, and sleeping on the sidewalk.

Does that mean we are going over the edge this time, or will the economy rebound and have us enjoy another eight or ten years of uninterrupted prosperity?

Strangely enough, the answer to that question, even though it may be somewhat important to us, is not as important to us personally as we may think.

What is important to us, really depends on whether it is us or our neighbor that happens to be working.

The rest of the country, or the world for that matter may be enjoying prosperity, but we could be in the middle of our personal "great depression." If we don't have an income and have no savings to pay our expenses, no matter what the economy is doing, we are in trouble.

And this is precisely where most of us make the mistake. We honestly believe that "it can't happen to us!"

And here is why.

When we start out in life, we are taught that if we get a proper education, get a good job with a well-known company, work hard and keep our nose to the grindstone, we will eventually reach our goals and enjoy all the goodies that money can buy.

We are also taught that if we make the right moves during our lifetime, we can become rich and enjoy a lifestyle of yachts, mansions, recognition, travel and leisure pursuits, and be independent of the daily work grind that befalls most mortals.

Unfortunately, most of us wind up slaving away all our lives and, in the end, wind up broke and deeply in debt.

And that is if we are lucky. If some really bad luck comes our way, regardless of our dreams and aspirations, we could wind up on the streets, begging for a meal every day.

The interesting thing is that no matter how high our current incomes happen to be - whether we are earning $50,000 or $500,000 annually - we are constantly faced with the same dilemma. That is, if we were to lose our source of income, our jobs or our businesses, and be without them for a sustained period of time (say a few months or a couple of years) we too could wind up on the streets.

Our conscious minds refuse to accept this fact as we enjoy all the goodies that our incomes are spoiling us with, but deep down inside we live in constant fear of losing our source of income and our attained lifestyle. This fear drives us to put in extra long hours and excessive effort into our jobs and professions, at the expense of our family relationships, our health and well being.

On the outside we appear happy, successful and prosperous with our fancy cars, luxurious homes, exotic vacations, but on the inside we are torn apart by the fear that all these toys that we have accumulated could be taken away from us at any moment.

We get into the trap of "A luxury once enjoyed becomes a necessity," and we identify ourselves with our job titles and the image that we project to the people around us. Our egos would be shattered if suddenly we could no longer be the Vice President of this or President of that, and Manager of the other or, if all of a sudden we had to sell our fancy car and our big house just to make ends meet.

We survive from day to day as prisoners of the public image we have created for ourselves, desperately protecting it at all costs.

Let's take a look at the story of Mr. and Mrs. Duckworth of Connecticut, and what it cost them to protect this image.

This is a real story.

According to a Wall Street Journal article, their net worth was, at its peak, about $3.4 million. Within a year it went down to zero.

Here is what happened.

Mr. Duckworth, a garment company executive earning multiple six figures, and Mrs. Duckworth, a housewife, had the fortune (or could it be the misfortune) of seeing their home and their beach house skyrocket in value from $25,000 to $600,000 each in 25 years.

When adding the equity value of the two properties, they became instant "millionaires."

Since millionaires deserve better things, they began accumulating better toys: big screen television sets, boats, his and hers Mercedes, and a duck-shaped telephone that quacked instead of ringing.

The major part of their spectacular net worth increase was due to inflated real estate values, so they perceived themselves as real estate tycoons.

They borrowed on their properties to make more real estate investments.

They decided to build another expensive beach house for speculation.

They also invested in a condominium development, becoming general partners on the project and naturally assuming the debts that went with the territory.

They were flying high and they felt that since they had gotten this far, it would be no problem getting even further in a shorter period of time.

It was like saying: "It's the end of the first inning and the Mets are winning one-nothing, therefore at the end of the ninth inning the Mets should be winning nine-nothing."

They forgot that there was the other team to contend with.

In their case, "the other team" represented the collapse of the real estate market in the Northeast. This left the Duckworths owing much more money than the values of their real estate holdings.

Since by this time Mr. Duckworth had also lost his job, the only alternative was to declare bankruptcy.

Were the Duckworths worried that their investments would not pan out as planned while all this was going on? I'll bet my last nickel that they were.

And what prevented them from taking a more cautious approach?

Perhaps they genuinely felt that they were providing a better life for themselves and their children by being reckless in their approach to business and personal finances. But I'll bet that same nickel on the fact that once they began enjoying all the goodies, their egos wouldn't let them pull back.

But we don't have to go all the way to Connecticut or raise $3.4 million of net worth to find a similar situation.

Every time we take on a bigger loan to trade in our Honda for a

Volvo, we go through the same thought process.

If you were to look back, say, ten years and remember your salary then and figure out how much you are earning today, you will probably be surprised at the big increase.

But what happened to all this money you earned in those years? How much of that money do you have left over and saved up in the bank? What happened to all those dollars?

And how about your debts? Are they more than what they were ten years ago?

Why is that so if you are earning so much more today?

If you lost your job, how long could you live on your savings?

How long could you pay your mortgage if your salary stopped and how long will it be before they took the house away unless you found another job quickly?

Do you remember the days when you were earning $2,000 a month and you used to say that if you only earned $3,000 monthly, all your financial problems would be solved? Then, when your income went to $40,000 per year, you said that if you could only earn $60,000 you would get yourself out debt and be on easy street.

But somehow it didn't work out that way. The more you earned, the bigger were your debts, and the more dependent you became on your income.

It really doesn't matter whether you are earning $50,000 or $100,000 or $500,000 annually, your expenses will magically expand with your income and you will become even more dependent on earning that income because your debts will expand in the same geometric proportion.

The sad truth is unless you recognize the problem and do something about it, you will be juggling your checkbook right up until you breathe your last breath.

So the first step in recognizing the problem is understanding that income is not wealth. No matter how expensive the toys are that you surround yourself with, you are not rich if you have to earn an income to maintain them.

Real wealth means the ability to live the way you want to without having to earn an income.

And the most amazing thing is that you really don't have to earn huge amounts of money or strike it rich in some clever business venture to accumulate enough capital within a reasonably short period of time to become independent of earned income. All you need to do is earn a middle-class standard of living and use your common sense in avoiding the traps that most people fall into, as did the Duckworths and as do most of us who ignore the forces that cause us to go broke.

Solvency is entirely a matter of temperament and not of income.

LOGAN PEARSALL SMITH, 1931

There is no art which one government sooner learns of another than that of draining money from the pockets of the people.

ADAM SMITH, 1776

No country has ever been ruined on account of its debts.

ADOLF HITLER, 1940

The worst country to be poor in is America.

ARNOLD TOYNBEE, 1954

No man divulges his revenue, or at least which way it comes in; but everyone publishes his acquisitions.

MICHEL DE MONTAIGNE, 1580

CHAPTER 3

Why not spend it all
and enjoy life?

REAL WEALTH IS NOT MEASURED in earned income nor the number of expensive toys with which we can surround ourselves. Instead, it represents the ability to maintain our present standard of living ad infinitum without having to earn an income.

That is the essence of "Financial Independence."

To reach this state, we must figure out how to outwit the forces that prevent us from achieving it.

What it takes is common sense, a little discipline, and the ability to conquer our ego.

But why should we go through this exercise? Why not just spend all the money we make as we go along and depend on the government or our company pensions to take care of us when we stop working?

The main reason is that we may be forced to stop working or our incomes may be substantially reduced, involuntarily, way before we are ready or eligible to receive our company or government benefits. Another reason is we may chose to stop producing the same income before those benefits kick in, and devote our energies to pursuits that may be much more personally rewarding and challenging yet may not produce the income we would need to maintain our lifestyle.

Every day, whether we are in our own business or are employed as managers or executives for someone else, we are faced with either losing our jobs or going out of business.

If we are in our own business, we have to worry about competition, economic downturns, costs of borrowing, obsolescence of our products or services, lawsuits, employee problems, and government regulation, just to name a few. Any one of those or a combination of them could put us out of business and, unless we have done something to prevent it, our business bankruptcy usually results in a personal bankruptcy.

Most business people have 75 percent or more of their net worth tied up in their businesses, and when a crisis occurs, they keep hanging on for dear life, even pouring in the remaining 25 percent of what they own to keep the business going until a turnaround happens. In most instances, the turnaround never happens and they wind up going down with the ship.

As an employee, the higher you go up the corporate ladder, the more money you earn, yet the more you spend in order to maintain the image that your position calls for. And the more difficult it becomes to land a comparable job. Yet as you get older, there are more and more younger, brighter, and more energetic people standing on the sidelines, ready to take over your job for much less pay and benefits. So unless you move up quickly, chances are you will be moving out.

The saddest thing to see is an executive, in his fifties, trying to keep up his image in the community, right after he has been terminated from his job. In the meantime, he has mortgages and college tuition to pay, as well as coping with the myriad of bills and obligations he has accumulated while he was "riding high."

It is very difficult for us to consciously consider the realities related to being "terminated."

In defense, we prefer to take the attitude of: "Who me? I am doing them a favor for being there. I can find a better deal anytime. Why, head hunters are calling me all day long and offering me positions sweeter than this one. They couldn't afford to lose me!"

Deep down inside we know we may be kidding ourselves but cannot allow those thoughts to creep to the surface. So we keep spending our salary, our bonus and our stock options as if we were going to be on the job forever. The more secure we appear on the surface, the more insecure we become on the inside, burying ourselves in our job at the expense of everything else in our life.

It may take our executive some time to recognize that he might not find a similar position soon, if ever, and that he should begin scaling down his spending patterns. But by that time, he had used up all his savings and was quickly going deeper into debt.

I have personally seen this scenario played out dozens of times but what amazes me is the answer I hear when I ask what the individual might have done to prepare for this situation. Invariably it is: "I never thought this could happen to me."

And this is exactly what I was thinking when this happened in my own life. But I'll talk about my story later.

So back to the question of "Why Financial Independence?"

In view of the above circumstances, being in a position of not having to be dependent on an income from your business or your job in order to maintain your lifestyle, to most of us, then becomes something worth attaining.

Qualitatively it means living a healthier, happier and longer life, without the illnesses caused by stress due to financial worries.

Financial Independence means:

You don't have to worry about losing your job or going bankrupt.

You don't have to put up with "idiot" co-workers or superiors. You can walk out at any time. Even though you may never walk out, just knowing that you don't have to stay there to keep the paycheck coming in is one heck of a stress reliever.

You can take as much time off as you want to and have the luxury of not having all your productive activities focused on "making money."

You can make career and professional choices based on that which you really enjoy and not necessarily based on how much money there is on the table.

You can be in control. You'll be in the position of giving ulcers, if that is what turns you on, and not getting them.

You will have the freedom of not being forced to work to just pay the bills.

But most important of all, you will become a much more effective executive or businessman because you won't have to be a "yes man" to your superiors or business associates just to please them and keep your job or the working relationship. You will be truly free to express your position exactly as you see it without having to water it down because it may not be consistent with someone else's view, someone with control over your position.

I'll never forget when I was a middle manager, sitting in a staff meeting, listening to my boss ramble on about some dumb idea, yet knowing that if I opened my mouth to tell him how I felt about it, I would be browbeaten into agreeing with him, and then as "punishment" for my honesty, being given some unpleasant assignment to deal with.

The Duckworth's may have been considered rich by some standards, but they were not wealthy because in spite of all the toys and the trappings, and the temporary high net worth, they never attained independence from earned income. And eventually, when their speculative ventures went sour, this fact came back to haunt them. They were very close to obtaining that independence, but in spite of all their good intentions they still stumbled over their egos.

You can see this pattern clearly with entertainers and professional managers.

If you were to scan the annual Forbes 400 wealthiest people in America, you will find that few, if any, entertainers or professional managers are on the list.

Have you wondered why Mr. Lee Iacocca, chairman of Chrysler, Mr. John Akers, chairman of I.B.M., Mr. Rand Araskog, chairman of ITT, and Mr. Robert Stampel, chairman of General Motors are not on the list? How about Frank Sinatra, Michael Jackson, Madonna and the rest of the big name entertainers? Why are they not on the list?

These respected scions of entertainment and industry have earned hundreds of millions of dollars during their careers. Perhaps even Billions. But where is their money?

It only takes a couple of hundred million dollars of net worth to make the Forbes 400 richest list. Some of the names I mentioned have earned that in just a few short years. But what happened to all those earnings?

Once again, here is proof that earned income is not wealth. I'll bet that if you were to take a close look at many of these "big earners," both entertainers and professional executives, you will probably find that if their incomes stopped, their investments couldn't sustain their living standard beyond a few years at best.

The difference between those individuals who are able to accumulate real wealth, and those that have huge earnings that slip right through their fingers, is those who kept their money knew how to deal with the forces that take it away while those who didn't, stumbled over their egos and lost it.

The problem is that we always seem to keep our appetites

salivating for a bigger car, a more expensive house, a bigger boat, and entry into a better club or neighborhood. Once there, we compete with the other neighbors.

For some reason we seem to think we're better than the guy next door if our stuff is more expensive than his.

Once we bite into this ego apple, we're hooked. We feel we can't do without it.

We refuse to recognize that the road to real wealth is the conversion of income to capital, and the creation and preservation of capital rather than chasing after income.

As a result of ignoring this reality, regardless of how much we make we are always juggling our checkbooks.

Just look at millionaires like Wayne Newton, Willie Nelson, George Gillete, The Hunts and others, who juggled and despite their millions of assets and income still went bankrupt.

Consider Robert Maxwell. When he died and the juggling stopped, there was no capital to provide an income to his family. Maxwell essentially was juggling a huge checkbook.

And as a result, with all his holdings and his yachts and his mansions, he never achieved financial independence. He became a prisoner of his personal trappings.

Many times I have heard the cop out to this viewpoint which goes something like this: "I love what I am doing and the way I am living. I really thrive on the pressure and the fast pace environment, and love the prestige that it gives me. I couldn't possibly be doing anything else. I'll make it and I'll spend it just as fast, and live to the limit! What is money good for except to enjoy it!"

But what they don't realize as that the downside to this cop out is, of course, the absence of peace of mind, loss of relationships with children, spouse and friends, poor health, an addiction to excesses and a loss of a true spiritual awareness.

The person that says that is usually not aware of the fact that he or she can have the work environment, all the toys you can play with and the financial independence to boot. You can really have your cake and eat it too if you do things right. Many have achieved it, and with a little adjustment in attitude, so can you.

But if those ageless reasons for creating real wealth are not enough, here are some current reasons why in today's economic environment, if we settle for the old cop out, we might be a lot worse off then we ever imagined.

Just a few short years ago, concern about staying ahead of our personal finances and achieving some degree of financial independence, may not have been an issue.

We were the most prosperous nation in the world. We could travel virtually anywhere, and find the countries we visited inexpensive (to us at least) to enjoy. The dollar was king and our savings and company retirement plans could easily take care of us when we stopped working and earning a living.

Virtually every family, regardless of their educational background could own their own home, have a couple of cars in the garage, and have the luxury of being a one earner family, with the husband pursuing a career and the wife taking care of the kids and the home as a housewife.

In those days, as long as we didn't go too deeply into debt, we could be assured that our company retirement, social security and our savings combined with the equity in our homes would take care of us in our twilight years.

Today, we face a completely different world.

It is virtually impossible for Americans to travel abroad like we used to because it is too expensive for us. The dollar has fallen behind other world currencies and our standard of living lags far behind most industrialized nations. Our medical care system is one of the worst, with our life expectancy one of the lowest and our infant mortality rate one of the highest in the world.

This means our older people are dying sooner than anywhere else and more of our babies die at birth than just about anywhere else. More than 40 million Americans have no medical coverage and more than 50 percent of households are two-earner families (with most younger families falling into that category) where the wife is no longer working to "buy some extras" but just to make ends meet.

Home ownership is virtually out of reach for most young Americans and "defined benefit" or "income" type retirement plans have been mostly replaced with 401K type plans which offer a mere fraction of the retirement benefits that the old plans used to provide.

For a period of more than thirty years, between 1940 and the early seventies, real incomes of the middle and lower classes of Americans have been steadily increasing, thus continuously raising our national standard of living. Over the last twenty years, the median income of the average American family has decreased in real terms by about 25 percent.

In the meantime, the wealthiest one percent, have more than doubled their real incomes during this period.

In addition, twenty years ago, 88 percent of the nation's wealth was held by 99 percent of the population. Today, 24 percent, of the wealth is held by the wealthiest 1 percent of the population, and the share of the wealth of the other 99 percent has slipped to 76 percent.

The rich are getting richer and the poor...much poorer.

In other words, we are slowly beginning to see a transformation of America from what was once a country made up primarily of a middle class that was prosperous and financially secure, to a nation that has a great disparity between the have's and have not's.

The middle class is slowly disappearing, and little by little we are becoming what we used think of as a typical "Banana Republic" with 5 percent very rich and 95 percent very poor.

We are not there yet, but at this rate, we may see this transformation become a reality within 30 or 40 years.

But there are conditions brewing that may accelerate this disparity between the rich and the poor, where we might see us as a nation of 5 percent rich and 95 percent poor much sooner.

One of those conditions exists right inside our own borders and the other relates to the recent break-up of the Eastern Block countries.

There is a third world country rapidly growing right inside America. The number of people living in ghettos below the poverty level is estimated to be over 30 million men, women, and mostly children.

That approximates the entire population of many countries in this world. And the numbers are growing! If we project the expansion of this poverty class over the next 20 years at, let's say 5 percent annual compounded growth per year, we are looking at almost 90,000 million people by 2012, and 130,000 million within 30 short years.

Since birth rates of the middle and upper classes have been declining, this could represent easily one third of our population living in slums. Many of them, as now, will be dealing in drugs, murder and other crimes, and generally living off the many state and federal public assistance program. The problem here is whether the other two thirds of the population will be able to afford or be willing to support the one third impoverished class. In order to accomplish this, taxes would have to be increased dramatically.

Can we afford this while even now we are running $400 billion annual budget deficits? In my opinion, increasing numbers of the poor will, in the future, be left to fend for themselves as they have been in other third world countries.

And those who are not so poor, will be spending greater amounts of their personal budgets to provide security in their neighborhoods to protect themselves from the increasing crimes originating from the increase in poverty.

These trends have already been put into place. Instead of spending tax dollars to eliminate the causes of poverty which in turn cause much of the crimes, the government is increasing budgets in the areas of law enforcement and crime control. And, in my opinion, this trend will continue.

Instead of legalizing drugs, we are pouring billions of dollars into the "War on Drugs" which ultimately results in billions of dollars of increased profits to the drug trade. Yet more than 50 percent of all crimes are drug related.

This stupid shortsightedness, will, in my opinion, accelerate the growth of poverty and aggravate the problem rather than relieving it.

As a result of the huge costs related to this approach, and the added tax burdens, more and more of today's middle class will cross over the poverty line, reducing the tax base while choking off profitable businesses and productive individuals.

Only the most profitable enterprises will survive, while most of the small businesses that have low profit margins and that represent much of our employment base will be negatively affected, placing even more individuals on the wrong side of that poverty line.

The breakup of the Eastern Block countries and the fall of Communism can also help accelerate the growth of poverty in our country.

Here is how.

For decades, we have been dependant on exporting our products to Europe and the Far East. This trade has kept our factories busy with orders and our factory workers employed and prosperous.

In recent years, Japan, Taiwan, Korea and Singapore have been cutting into our internal markets and have confronted us with formidable competition abroad to the detriment of our own economy.

Fortunately for us, Japan, Taiwan, Korea and Singapore no

longer represent cheap labor, making our products more competitive on world markets.

The Eastern Block countries are another story. The former Soviet Union, today has many more graduate engineers, scientists, and other technically-trained individuals than we do. And they are willing to work for practically nothing. At today's exchange rates, the average Russian engineer with a graduate degree will earn $8 per month.

Under the communist system, the bureaucracy made manufacture of various products both inefficient and lacking in quality.

Now, however, under the free enterprise system, it will be a different story.

Within the next few years, we will see world markets flooded with goods manufactured and assembled in these former Eastern European countries.

The quality will be good and the prices low. Much lower than what we, or for that matter Japan, Taiwan, Korea and Singapore, can produce.

For that reason, many European and Pacific Rim manufacturers are currently setting up twin plant assembly operations for their products in those Eastern countries.

Soon we could see a flood of television sets, V.C.R.'s, Cam Corders, automobiles and other items coming out of those countries at half the price we make them for in the U.S.

This will further depress our manufacturing sector, impacting unemployment and accelerating the spiral toward an ever increasing poverty class.

Our multi-national manufacturers will profit handsomely as they assemble more and more goods in Eastern Block countries and fewer and fewer goods in the U.S., leaving more workers here without their job. Smaller companies that do not have the resources to set up twin plant operations will go out of business, adding to the spiral in unemployment.

A recent study was made by Regional Financial Associates, Inc. projected the loss to our G.N.P., as related to defense cut backs of the "peace dividend," to be an average of 2 percent over the next 7 years.

When we add to this the loss of jobs related to lost world markets as a results of the much cheaper labor in those Eastern Block countries, the loss to our G.N.P. could be even greater. And this will accelerate the gap between rich and poor.

The thinking of yesteryear which espoused the principles of hard work and frugality that would assure us a secure financial future may be totally inappropriate for the year 2000 and beyond.

We have to think and do things differently than we ever did before if we are to be part of the 5 percent well-to-do rather than part of the 95 percent poor.

In these times, just being part of the middle working class is not enough. If all we do is try to maintain the status quo, we will soon be joining the ranks of the poor. And if we don't recognize this, we will be in for a rude awakening as we too, slowly, almost imperceptibly, slip into poverty.

The real question is: "Over the next 20 years, if the scenario does play out as I have described it, are we going to be the 5 percent with a secure financial future, or are we going to be part of the army of the 95 percent who don't know from day to day where their next meal is coming from?

So unless we strive to achieve some degree of Financial Independence, while we can, we may never get a chance later.

The rich get richer and the poor get poorer.

ANDREW CARNEGIE, 1900

The U.S. is the fastest "undeveloping" country in the world.

ARTHUR LAFFER, 1979

We'll hold the distinction of being the only nation in the history of the world that ever went to the poorhouse in an automibile.

WILL ROGERS, 1932

*Nobody ever saw a dog make a fair and deliberate exchange
of one bone for another with another dog.*

ADAM SMITH, 1776

*These capitalists generally act harmoniously and in concert,
to fleece the people.*

ABRAHAM LINCOLN, 1837

*For what is a man profited, if he
shall gain the whole world,
and lose his own soul.*

MATTHEW 16:26, c A.D. 80

Competing and striving to be "number one" may feed our ego, but it's bad for our pocketbook

WHAT HAS ALWAYS BEEN VERY AMUSING to me is the emphasis that is placed in this country on "beating the competition," "winning," "being the best," "overcoming your opponent," "measuring up," etc.

This attitude has permeated not only the business environment but touches our lives at every juncture.

Our relationships with our friends, our spouses, our children, our coworkers, and our colleagues are in some way or another expressed in one form of competitive spirit or another.

Just take a look at our most popular pastimes. Football, boxing, tennis, baseball, along with a garden variety of sports whose only object is to beat the other guy.

We seem to be constantly ready to go to war with anybody who offers us a challenge.

We thrive on the feeling of "being the champion." Somehow, being labeled "second best" carries with it a shame that hurts us deeper than perhaps anything else.

We thrive on that terrible emotion "pride." We give up our lives for it, then we wonder why we are broke and unhappy.

The problem with competition is that in order to compete, you have to have an enemy. In my experience, sometimes whomever or whatever we initially perceive to be the enemy may, in fact, turn out to be our best friend.

But because we are conditioned to "compete" and "win," we many times lose sight of opportunities to become part of our object of competition and, as a result of this merger, grow and become better and more prosperous individuals.

We waste our energies on beating out the other guy rather than figuring out how we can best take advantage of the situation, work with him and as a result, create a synergistic effect that would get us much more rewarding results than if we stood alone.

Once again, our egos which in this case manifest themselves as "pride in our posessions and accomplishments" get in the way of the most productive decisions.

We begin this destructive process by first deciding who will be "with us" in our lifetimes and who will be "against us."

And if they are not "with us," then, to our way of thinking, they must be "against us" and therefore they become an opponent that needs to be dealt with and perhaps eliminated.

This process of first deciding who is on our side and then identifying the enemy followed by eliminating this enemy, requires an incredible amount of negative energies to execute. These energies are not used to add to our personal well being but, on the contrary, sap us of the power we posses to make our lives better and more productive, both financially and spiritually.

We have all heard the expression: "If you can't beat them, join them." Why not modify it to: "Since it doesn't pay to beat them, let's join them."

The spiritual part I am going to leave to others who are much more qualified than I to expound on the subject, because that is not the focus of this book. However, since I have been in the business of personal finance for over thirty years, that is an area where I feel I can speak with some authority.

And based on this personal experience, I can say this. If you want to make money in business or in whatever field your expertise may lie, and then get to keep it, you don't want to be competitive! This process of competition and fighting to become "number one" will lead you straight to the poorhouse.

Mao Tse Tung had an interesting philosophy on winning wars. He said simply: "When the enemy attacks you retreat and when the enemy retreats you attack."

That is the first lesson. You don't waste your energies by meeting your "competition" head on.

You need to use those energies instead to find out where you can go so that you don't need to deal with an "enemy," and if no matter where you go, this "enemy" persists, you need to figure out how you can make this enemy your friend. You will be surprised to learn that chances are, he probably wants the same thing.

And once you find your "enemiesless" arena, you can channel your energies into those things that enhance your life rather than those that sap your energies through negative pursuits.

I encountered this "winning/loser" syndrome in many instances where I would hire former athletes as insurance and securities salespeople. They would usually do very well in sales because of their public image, but because of this ingrained brainwashing about competition and winning, their personal and financial lives were a total disaster.

They would focus so much on winning a plaque in a sales contest, they would forget to take care of the things that were very close to their own lives, like their families, their investments, their spending patterns, and their relationships with their friends and coworkers.

It was great for me because I made my money on overrides from the sales they made. But for them, it represented throwing away their lives for a lousy plaque.

It is this type of manipulative brainwashing about winning and competition that can leave a former professional athlete almost a virtual cripple as far as functioning effectively in the "outside world."

And it is this same brainwashing that makes this very athlete a prize for anyone who is willing to exploit what I call his or her "mental disability for winning" for their own personal gain.

The reason that I relate so very well to the above statement is because at different points in my life I had stood on both sides of the fence.

As a biathlon skier, I became a "winning" machine. And later, as an executive in the insurance and securities business, I learned very well how to use other athlete's "mental disabilities" to my advantage.

As I mentioned earlier, before you can begin to compete, you first have to identify who it is that you are going to compete against. That is, you have to find your "enemy."

I first began to get an inkling to the fact there is no such thing as an enemy back in 1971, when I was thirty years old.

The incident occurred when I was at the home office of the insurance company I represented in Puerto Rico, attending a cocktail party.

I was in conversation with a very nice fellow General Agent who we will call Gordon for the purpose of this story.

He appeared a little sloshed, which was no surprise because we had all had an intense day in a special orientation seminar and most of us had a little too much to drink.

He asked me where I was from and I told him that I was born in Yugoslavia of Georgian parents.

Because my agency was in Puerto Rico, I immediately became his Puerto Rican/Georgian friend. He seemed to have found humor in the combination.

He immediately told me that he was very familiar with Yugoslavia because he used to fly bombing missions into Belgrade from England during the Second World War. Yugoslavia was under the German occupation at that time, the purpose of the missions was to get the Germans out.

As he got into his story, he became very excited about describing to me those missions in great detail.

At that moment, the room where I was and the merry crowd in it suddenly disappeared for me and I was back in Belgrade in my grandfather's house. I was four years old and it was 1945.

I remember hearing the air raid sirens wailing and the loudspeakers that were attached to lamp posts calling out in German, "Achtung! Achtung!", warning the residents to seek shelter.

These were Allied bombers which were to drop bombs on the Germans to get them out.

But, since back then there were no smart bombs that could identify national origins, we all had to run for cover.

I remember my Aunt grabbing me and carrying me to the garage where some neighbors had gathered along with many members of our family including aunts, uncles, and cousins.

The garage was the place where, for some reason, everybody felt safer than in the house. This was our family "bomb shelter."

The garage was dark and I couldn't see very much, but I remember some people sitting on the floor and others on makeshift stools. There was a goat tied to one of the stools and a couple of dogs running around and barking. I sat on my Aunt's lap listening to the whine of the approaching bombs and the far away thuds as they exploded somewhere else. I knew even then that if you didn't hear the thud after the whine, you were in trouble, that bomb had your name on it.

I suddenly snapped back and there was Gordon once again standing in front of me recounting his stories about missions into Yugoslavia.

He kept talking about liberating the "Slobs." I am sure he meant "Slavs," but I think it was the fourth martini that must have been keeping his tongue twisted.

He told me how this was the end of the war, and the only reason he was alive now and talking to me was because he was smart and didn't act like some other dumb heroes who didn't make it.

He said when he flew missions, he wouldn't risk his life like the other "dummies" by bombing military targets. That's where they had anti-aircraft guns that could knock down a plane very easily. He told me they would just simply fly into Belgrade, and dump the bombs in the suburbs, and hightail it back to England with a "mission accomplished" report.

I was catapulted back to my grandfather's garage once again and the sounds of the bombs exploding all around us.

Then suddenly it was quiet. I looked up and it was no longer dark in the garage. I saw the sky and some people standing on top trying to tie some ropes to climb down. There was smoke and dust all around. I could only move my head; the rest of my body was immobile. I felt a warm liquid pouring on my face. I turned my head and saw my Aunt's neck, with the head severed from it and veins protruding and pouring her blood all over me.

In an instant I was back in Hartford. I looked at Gordon but could not hear a word he was saying. I wanted to throw up.

I thought to myself: "Who is the enemy?"

Is it Gordon because it was his bombs that might have wiped out half my family?

Was it the Germans who created the condition for Gordon to be there in the first place?

Was it Gordon because he had the presence of mind to try to save his own life where others, who didn't do the same thing he did, might have been dead? Can you blame someone for trying to save his own life?

Or was it the Allies, who, in their zeal to get the Germans out, were slaughtering millions of innocent human beings.

Folks, there is no enemy! And if there is no enemy then there is no one to compete with or get even with.

That's when I knew that the only way to come out a winner in this world was not to fight them. All you have to do is love them to death. Competition is for losers!

Somebody much smarter than me said this a couple thousand years ago, so who am I to argue with that philosophy!

Let us be grateful to Adam our benefactor. He cut us out of the "blessing" of idleness and won for us the "curse" of labor.

MARK TWAIN, 1910

Work is the refuge of people who have nothing better to do.

OSCAR WILDE, 1897

They talk of the dignity of work. Bosh. The dignity is in leisure.

HERMAN MELVILLE, 1849

Business or toil is merely utilitarian. It is necessary, but does not enrich or enable a human life.

ARISTOTLE, c. 360 B.C.

As a rule, from what I've observed, the American captain of industry doesn't do anything out of business hours. When he has put the cat out and locked up the office for the night, he just relapses into a state of coma from which he emerges only to start being a captain of industry again.

P.G. WODEHOUSE, 1925

All work and no play makes Jack a dull boy.

JAMES HOWELL, 1659

The law of work does seem utterly unfair, but there it is, and nothing can change it: the higher the pay in enjoyment the worker gets out of it, the higher shall be his pay in cash also.

MARK TWAIN, 1889

Hard work and dedication to your career will lead you straight to the poorhouse!

IN MY OPINION, ONE OF THE BIGGEST OBSTACLES to attaining financial independence is hard work.

Somehow the harder we seem to work, the more we become slaves to our routines and our habits and the more we are forced to keep our noses to the grindstone.

As a result, instead of focusing on the end result we want to achieve, we pay too much attention to the details of our work routine, making us more efficient, but much less effective in reaching our goals. We miss the big opportunities because we focus on the little tasks.

But worst of all, we begin to lose perspective of our total life and begin to view our life from the narrow viewpoint of our profession or business.

We become focused on "getting the job done" and forget that the real job is our life and not our work. Our work is only one tiny fraction of our life, yet the harder we work, the more we base our life decisions on our professional and business goals.

Then, when we realize our entire life centers around our work, we cop out with the following oxy-moron: "My life is my work."

Sounds noble, but while it may work for Robots, for us Human Beings it just doesn't cut it.

What puzzles me is how and when did we civilized folks come to regard hard work as a virtue?

Granted, we do have to put an effort into our businesses and professions to make them successful. We have a need to express ourselves professionally and achieve success and recognition by our peers. That is good fodder for the ego, and by no means am I putting down this aspect of work dedication.

What I am referring to are compulsive work habits that we display as a badge, which end up denying us our personal development and rob us of our time for ourselves and our families.

How many times have we heard someone declare proudly: "I haven't taken a vacation in five years!" or "I never put in less than 60 or 70 hours per week!" or "I can't take time off now because I am in the middle of an important project!" or "I haven't missed a day from work in 10 years!"

Some are even proud to say: "I am a workaholic!"

These statements are made as if we should applaud this self destructive behavior.

From my viewpoint, anyone who thinks this way will have a very tough time achieving financial independence because he or she is so bogged down in the details of their work that they can't see where they are going. They "can't see the forest for the trees."

In other words, they totally miss the big picture of life, and as a result, become slaves to their compulsive work habits.

Unfortunately, this ridiculous work-ethic nonsense has permeated our thoughts for so long that we are made to feel guilty if we don't work ourselves to death.

And for what? A plaque to gather dust on the wall? A gold watch at retirement? The promotion that goes to someone else because of politics? To make an extra $10,000 or $100,000 or even a million dollars in profits for a business that will eventually wind up in somebody else's hands anyway? Or maybe we are looking for an approving pat on the head by our superiors as if to say: "That's a good dog, Fido".

How many times have we skipped events that were important-a child's graduation, a planned vacation, a weekend with the family, helping one of the kids solve a problem, or just time off to goof off-by excusing ourselves and saying: "I have to work!"

When we do this we are basing our decision on the erroneous assumption that we have to be there or that things won't go smoothly without us.

Don't flatter yourself! If you took the next couple of weeks off, no matter how critical the moment, things would get done somehow.

NO one is indispensable, not even the boss. Vacuums get filled, but it doesn't boost our egos to think of ourselves as a vacuum.

Here are some of the most common lies we tell ourselves to justify our workaholic habits. If you see yourself using any of those lies, why don't you ask yourself the questions that follow the lie?

"I'm doing this to make a better life for my family!"

What does your family really want?

"In this world, you have to be the best you can be and compete at all times even if it means personal sacrifice to achieve business and professional goals!" Do you really know what your personal goals are?

"I need to set an example for my subordinates!" How do you know that they are watching or even that they care one hoot about what you do?

"They are counting on me!" Who is counting on you and if you weren't there, how do you know that someone else couldn't do it better than you?

"If I work real hard, I'll get everything I ever wanted in life!" What do you really want and how do you know that your actions will really lead you to it? More important, how do you really know that someone is watching and cares about what you do to give it to you?

"I am building a better future!" How do you know that now is not your future?

I could go on but I think you've got the picture. The name of the game is not to work hard but to work smart.

I learned this lesson just a little bit too late for me to have saved my first marriage but not too late to make my life a little bit better afterward. As a result, my ex-wife and I have been great friends over the years and my children, who were small at the time of our divorce, have been very close to me during their later years.

Especially after I had an opportunity to be a single parent when my youngest son Michael was eleven and my older son Sasha was fifteen.

To understand my transition, I need to give you a little bit more background.

Right after I was discharged from the U.S. Army, I was all of twenty-one years old and my son Sasha was born. I needed a job. So where does an aspiring young high school drop-out go to find a job in a hurry?

You got it! When you are unemployable you can always try the Insurance Business. God bless America!

So I started as a debit collector for a major insurance company in an area called East New York, Brooklyn. My assignment was to collect insurance premiums from welfare recipients who lived in the low-income projects and the tenements in the area. For those of you who are not familiar with either the area or the process of collection, here is how it worked.

I walked around with a big book in my hand and went to collect money from residents. While I was there I sold them more insurance that was to be paid weekly.

Now, that wouldn't have been so bad except for the fact that by walking around with a big book, all the neighborhood hoodlums knew you were collecting money so you became a target. When you went into the elevator of one of the projects, a couple of hoodlums would jump in there with you, press the stop button, and tell you that you had their wallet in your pocket.

The problem was that I was responsible personally for all the money that was collected, and I could see quickly that if I continued to comply with their requests, I would go broke.

So I went out and got myself a lead pipe. Problem solved! From that point on, I was known as "the man with the lead pipe." Of course, today, I wouldn't stand a chance because they all have guns. But those were the good old easy days. That's high tech progress for you!

Anyway, I really had no alternatives and no place else to go. This job was to be my road to riches so I hung in there.

Perhaps that was another bit of good fortune that had befallen me. I had few options to "make it," so that meant I had to make the best of what I had. I had to do it!

Well, I worked very long hours and progressed into management. Then a better opportunity presented itself with another major insurance company. I took it, and within a few short years I was breaking all kinds of records in the insurance business. In no time, my unit of salespeople became number one in the company and after a brief stint in the Home Office as a director of training, I was appointed as Agency Manager of a plush Manhattan office at 55 Madison Avenue. I was twenty-eight at the time, and was the youngest Agency Manager ever to be appointed by that company.

The problem was that by this time my second son Michael was born, and I hadn't seen my kids or my wife in years. Not literally, of course, but just because I was occasionally there in body, it didn't mean that I was really there in spirit.

I was totally focused on "Success" with a huge "S."

My marriage was in total shambles and I didn't know who my kids were, but I was "Master of the Universe."

Since my wife was from Puerto Rico, and erroneously thinking that moving my family closer to her relatives would save the marriage, I accepted an offer from another major company to begin a new operation there. Within a year of our move, my wife and I were divorced. It wasn't the geography that needed changing. It was me, but I didn't know it yet.

In just a few short years, my agency became the biggest such operation in Puerto Rico, and one of the biggest in the company. My walls were heavy with plaques and awards that I had won during those years, and I was giving speeches all over the country about my over-achievements.

But that still wasn't enough.

A friend of mine from Texas called me one day and asked if I would join him and a couple of other people in taking over a group of small life insurance companies that were in a marketing rut.

I jumped at the chance and, lo and behold, at the age of thirty five I was president and chairman and major stockholder of a small life insurance company. Between the stock that was given to me as part of the deal and the options on additional stock, I became an instant millionaire. In those days, before inflation, a million dollars was a lot of money. But the worst part was that I believed it and lived like it.

Up to that point, my insurance career had been a meteoric ride straight up. I thought I was invincible, but the worst part was that I truly believed there would be no end to this success.

Two and a half years later, I came back to Puerto Rico after being fired from my job by the board with my tail between my legs, a very much bruised ego, and broke. (How could the President get fired? Easy, it happens all the time!)

I was thirty-seven years old then, and it was the best thing that had ever happened to me.

Fortunately, the agency operation that I had left behind was practically down to nothing and they welcomed me back with open arms to take it over again.

This gave me an awful lot of time to reflect on my life.

Probably the most significant flashback that helped me change my life around was, surprisingly enough, a motivational movie that was made many years ago about a famous football coach who, during his lifetime had become a legend. In the movie, this coach kept talking about the sacrifice and the dedication that one has to go through in order to become a champion. The movie kept showing football players going through thousands of drills in order to perfect certain techniques. It talked about the fact that to be a champion, one had to dedicate himself totally to the profession and have no outside distractions and influences. One had to be totally committed to winning because, in his words, "WINNING IS NOT EVERYTHING, IT IS THE ONLY THING!"

As he said those words, the camera focused on his face and in the background he had a display of all the trophies he had won.

When I saw this man's face in my flashback, I realized how pathetic he had looked. Here was this old man, talking about winning being everything and it was clear to see that the only thing that meant anything to him in his life was the stack of trophies that he had accumulated.

"And there, but for the grace of God go I," I thought to myself. I saw myself in front of my wall of trophies, looking pathetic and talking about winning, and that's when I knew that this coach, who was larger than life, had no clue to what this life was all about.

I thought about all those young people that bought that ridiculous philosophy of "competitiveness," and "being a winner" and "dedication at all costs" and how they had thrown their life away for a few years of glory on the football field, just to give some pathetic old man an extra plaque to hang on the wall. And for what? To spend the rest of their lives physically broken up, rejected, thrown away like some old rag after they were no longer young enough and strong enough to carry the ball? To me then, the game of football, which has so many parallels to the game of business, brought to mind a clear picture of: "LIONS TWO, CHRISTIANS NOTHING!"

That flashback reminded me of one of my best friends when I lived in Dallas, a famous kicker for the Dallas Cowboys, and the frustration and the heartache he had gone through as he was approaching the twilight years of his career. He dedicated his whole life to the game. Then, when he began approaching forty and they no longer needed him, he was dumped. He was a committed and dedicated winner, and look what it got him.

At that point I realized that the best way to make it through life in one piece and come out a real "winner" was to take the approach to business like the Kamikaze pilot who flew twelve missions. He was committed, but he wasn't totally involved.

I came to this realization my first day back in Puerto Rico. I decided to take a walk on the beach early that morning before going to the office. I'll never forget my thoughts as I walked by one of the hotels.

I said to myself: "I'll give this thing two years, but I am going to focus on what is important to me and not to somebody else. My personal well being would come before money, success and ego. No more hard work and dedication. And if I couldn't make it that way, I would take tourists out on my hobie cat or give windsurfing lessons. If I couldn't make it as a businessman, I knew I would be successful as a forty year old beach bum."

I faced the abyss, and was willing to risk going down into it. I finally let go!

I realized that this time around I had better do things differently. And that's when I formulated my personal philosophy on life:

"WINNING IS NOTHING BUT ENJOYING THE GAME OF LIFE IS EVERYTHING!"

And I did!

Since my kids were now getting a little older, my ex-wife and I decided that it would be a good experience for them and for me to have them living with me. Every man should experience being a single parent.

I also decided that my priorities would no longer be focused on success and making money, but on other things.

The amazing thing that happened was that even though my approach to business was now totally different, my insurance agency grew even faster than before. Within three years, we were once again within the top ten in the company and the largest in Puerto Rico. We quickly expanded, and grew to 160 producers and eight sales managers all over Puerto Rico and the Virgin Islands. I added other lines of business to our operations, including a Broker/Dealership where we were also selling securities and special tax-sheltered programs.

But the difference now was that I was taking at least six weeks vacation every year, and you could find me at the beach two or three afternoons per week sailing my Hoblie Cat or windsurfing.

I never worked weekends, and my work week usually didn't exceed thirty or thirty-five hours. But the biggest reward of all was to finally having gotten to know my kids. My kids moving in with me was the best thing that happened to me and I strongly recommend to every divorced male to be a "single parent" for a while. It does wonders to your attitude! That was worth everything!

Since I now had more time on my hands, I could pay more attention to my personal finances. I set some goals and, because my head was clear, could stick to them. I gained control of my personal spending patterns and investment objectives, and pretty soon my net worth was increasing by leaps and bounds.

I had finally gotten off the merrygoround and was in control of my life!

There is one point I would like to clarify. In the first chapter I mentioned that my earnings never exceeded $100,000 annually. So the first question that you may be asking is: "If you had all this success in the insurance business, how come you earned so little money?"

The answer to that is in the nature of operating as a "General Agent" in the insurance business. That is, you get your overrides not in the year that you brought in the business, but they are sometimes spread over two or three years and in some cases over the next ten years. So if you stay put, you eventually collect them, and if you jump to a better opportunity with more potential, you have to give up what you have built up.

In my case, since I skipped from one opportunity to the next relatively quickly, I was never there long enough to collect all the overrides that were coming to me. In other words, I gave up current income for an opportunity with greater potential.

When I became a C.E.O. of an insurance company, my salary was close to $100,000 annually back in 1976, but my serious money, I figured, would come from the company stock that was offered to me as part of the deal.

Since that situation turned out to be a disaster for me, I never collected on the stock.

With the insurance company I represented in Puerto Rico, my real profit came from ownership of the renewal overrides on the business that we were doing which were spread over ten years.

So even though my annual earned income was below $100,000, eventually I collected the present value of those renewals in a lump sum after I retired from the insurance business.

And, I should add, that "capital," even though by itself would not have been enough, but when added to my other assets made a big difference in my reaching financial independence. The most important lesson, to me, from this experience has been: "Don't chase after income. Go for the opportunity to build capital even if it means less income." Just think of it this way: "It is a lot easier to earn $100,000 than to save $100,000."

I started this chapter talking about the evils of hard work. Here is my personal recipe as to how one can shake that terrible, compulsive habit.

• If you run your own business, take a calendar and scratch out two or three months, allocating them to vacation or other personal projects. If you are an employee or executive, scratch out all the vacation time you are entitled to and stick to it. Don't let a business emergency derail your plans.

PAY YOURSELF FIRST WITH YOUR PERSONAL TIME.

• Do not allow business commitments to interfere with important personal projects. Don't cancel an afternoon of windsurfing, tennis or golf because of a pressing meeting. Be as strict with your personal time as you are with you business time, and don't apologize for it. Be proud of it!

• Eliminate "should" and "ought to" from your vocabulary. Only do what you feel is right for the situation, making sure it is your decision and not a concession to someone or something else.

• Call in "well" occasionally. That's right. Most of us call in sick to take an unscheduled day off. Why not just take the day off when you feel great and want to do something other than go to work? Don't apologize, just say "I'm feeling fantastic and I'm taking my kids to the ballgame! Cancel all my appointments."

Others may get angry with you initially, but believe it or not, you will get respect because everyone will love to be like you.

If you think this attitude will ruin your business or your career, think again. Six months of recovery after a heart attack could do a lot more damage.

All of this is to say: "It is most important that work is placed in it's proper perspective." We work in order to provide cash flow to live and create wealth, and to experience some personal challenge. However, any effort beyond that is totally unnecessary. And any dedication or commitment to work that would take precedence over the really important things in life, like your family and your personal physical and mental well being, is in my opinion, absolutely preposterous and ridiculous.

If you are an employer, you may want your employees to develop a workaholic attitude. It may be in your best interest as an employer that the people who work for you, give up much of their personal lives and devote that time to your business so that you can make more profit. You may want to create an atmosphere of pride in hard work and a feeling of guilt by those employees who do not put in the extra hours and effort.

Just look at the Japanese. Most employees in Japan take half the vacations they are allowed and regularly stay slaving away behind their desks well after quitting time. If they don't, they are ostracized by their employers and coworkers. The result? The corporations they work for are strong, profitable and efficient. Yet the employees' personal lives are a shambles. They spend little time in personal pursuits and few break out of the rat race to become entrepreneurs themselves. There is a high degree of suicide attributed to workaholic habits in Japan and in the end, this attitude can backfire on the employer through eventual loss of productivity.

In summary, if you are going to put in the extra work effort, make sure you are doing it for yourself and not for someone else. Pay yourself first; whether it may be with leisure time or with your work dedication. But put your personal well being well ahead of your work responsibilities.

Few people do business well who do nothing else.

LORD CHESTERFIELD, 1749

He that will make a good use of any part of his life must allow a large part of it to recreation.

JOHN LOCKE, 1690

We have had somewhat too much of the "gospel of work". It is time to preach the gospel of relaxation.

HERBERT SPENCER, 1882

Never spend your money before you have it.

THOMAS JEFFERSON, 1813

The larger the income. the harder it is to live within it.

RICHARD WHASTELY, 1832

*Thrift is the great fortune-maker. It draws the line between the savage
and the civilized man.*

ANDREW CARNEGIE, 1900

*I do want to get rich but I never want to
do what there is to do to get rich.*

GERTRUDE STEIN, 1937

CHAPTER 6

A little discipline
can be painless

SO FAR, I HAVE TOUCHED on some internal forces that work against us and which can prevent us from attaining our financial goals. They include attitudes that I feel are crucial to develop if you want to attain Financial Independence.

In a nutshell, in order for me to have gained what I felt was a proper perspective on life, I had to make a conscious decision not to work hard but to work "smart;" to take an exorbitant amount of time off for leisure pursuits and not feel guilty about it; to be loyal to myself and my family and not to some other entity such as my employer or my job or my profession; to understand what it is that I wanted and especially what it was that I really "needed"; to not allow my ego to cloud my good judgement; and essentially not to worry about winning the game of life but concentrate on enjoying the process of playing it.

I did not finally "get it all together" - where my life reflected the principles I describe in the above paragraph - until my late thirties. After that it took me less than ten years to reach the point where I no longer needed to depend on an income to live the way I wanted to live for an indefinite period of time.

But attitude is only one piece of this puzzle. Another and possibly much more important part, is discipline.

Most people seem to have the erroneous idea that discipline means repeatedly forcing yourself to do an unpleasant task for a sustained period of time. Nothing could be further from the truth. If you have to force yourself to do something, it probably isn't worth doing.

The approach I take to anything I do, whether it is personal or professional, is:

"IF IT'S FUN TO DO I'LL DO IT. IF NOT, I'LL FORGET IT."

I don't like to grind away at unpleasant tasks, so I just avoid them.

Most students of the protestant work ethic would be appalled at this attitude, so if you fall into this category, pay attention. There may be an important lesson here for you.

My most profound brush with discipline was thrust on me while I was in the U.S. Army.

As an immigrant, you are the first in line to get drafted. So, shortly after I crossed the border into the good old U.S.A. I got my "Greetings" notice. That was in June of 1961. I was nineteen years old.

After the usual basic training I was sent to Fairbanks, Alaska for permanent duty. By the time September rolled around, winter was in full swing, and I was placed in an infantry platoon whose job was to test equipment under extreme conditions. Whenever the temperature would go down to 60 or 70 degrees below zero, we would get packed off in helicopters to exotic places within the Arctic circle like Point Barrow, Nome, or some other God forsaken stretch of ice and snow. We were given tents, ahkios (sleds that were pulled by people), gasoline for heaters to stay warm, C rations for food, a couple of clips of live ammo to keep away the moose and the bears, and told to survive until they got back to us a couple of weeks later.

Now don't get me wrong. It wasn't that bad. As a matter of fact at age nineteen, to me this was the epitome of adventure. Especially since I had voraciously devoured all the works by Jack London (in Russian) while I was a kid.

The problem was when they finally did pick us up and brought us back to the barracks in Fairbanks to thaw out, they would count the toes and fingers and other parts of the body to see how they were effected by frostbite. The idea was that if 92 percent of the fingers came back intact, the gloves we used that week were better than the week before, because only 79 percent of the fingers which used last week's gloves were still functioning.

Even though I loved the adventure, I had somehow placed an

extraordinary value on certain parts of my body. So when an opportunity came up to find a more compatible line of work with my anatomy, I applied for it.

This opportunity manifested itself in the form of an announcement on the barracks bulletin board about tryouts for the Biathalon Team. I had no idea what Biathatlon meant at the time, but at that juncture, anything seemed like a step in the right direction.

It turned out that Biathalon was an Olympic sport that included cross country skiing and firing at targets with a rifle.

About two hundred applicants came from all over the country to tryout for the few empty slots they had on the team. Since I had never skied before I got to Alaska, I was a little apprehensive. But the system was very simple. They did not want to know what your skiing skills were. The only thing that mattered was endurance. They would give us all the training we needed later if we managed to get on the team. A couple of hundred of us started going around a fifteen-mile trail. At the end of the day, the two who got the job were the two still left skiing after everyone else dropped out.

The selection process was quite uncomplicated.

The interesting thing was that the other qualifier for the team was also someone who had never skied before, a Mexican-American from Bakersfield, California called Sam. Sam and I later became good friends.

From that day on, my whole life in the Army changed. I lived off post. I seldom wore a uniform. And my only duty was to stay in good physical shape for the competitions which meant skiing about 40 or 50 miles per day on cross-country ski trails.

For a nineteen year old, I thought I had died and gone to heaven. But what does all this have to do with discipline, you may ask? I am coming to that.

Reading this story, you may think of me as some kind of super Olympic athlete or something. Nothing could be further from the truth. In fact, I had always been sickly as a child, suffering asthma and other afflictions.

When I was in high school, I was never good at sports. I was clumsy, uncoordinated, and didn't really have much strength because I was too skinny.

Physical activity was definitely not my strong point!

It took me a few years to realize what really transpired during those Biathalon tryouts. Here you had a gathering of fine athletes who were excellent skiers, had years of experience, proper diet and training, exercise, and so on and who felt they rightly belonged on the team.

However, even though they had all the physical attributes that I didn't have, I had something that they didn't. I had a motive.

I just didn't want to come back to the barracks one day without my fingers or my toes or for that matter, my nose. It was that simple. They merely wanted to be on the team. I wanted to enjoy my extremities for a little while longer. My motive was stronger than theirs. With that kind of motivation, ordinary people are capable of accomplishing the most extraordinary things. And that's all it was. Me, a plain ordinary wimp, with a motive, against super athletes who, really didn't have one. A simple contest of mind over brawn. The mind, invariably, wins. That was an important lesson for me although I didn't know it at the time.

I think that those of you who are long distance runners can probably understand and relate to the process very easily. When your body reaches a certain point of exhaustion where you feel deep in your bones you cannot take one single step more, the mind suddenly takes over. If you are able to cross that threshold, suddenly a new strength seems to come out of nowhere and takes hold of you. You feel separated from your body and actually feel that you are an observer floating above and watching your own body skiing along the trail.

At that point you know for a fact that your body is not really you. You also know you have total control to keep running your body until it dies. And you know that if your body dies, you will continue. It is a very spiritual experience that gives you a glimpse of your own immortality. You know that your body can drop dead, but you'll still be there. For a brief moment you come face- to-face with your own spirit!

But this is taking us off the subject. Back to discipline.

Discipline, then, is nothing more than having the proper motive. Most people beat their head against the wall, forcing themselves to do things they don't like doing and feeling very virtuous for this effort. I feel this is a ridiculous waste of energy.

The name of the game is to reach deep down inside yourself and find a motive for your actions. Visualize the end result that you want to achieve and allow that motive to excite you and take hold of you.

Your body will then somehow automatically begin doing things in order for you to reach this end result. You will then no longer be forcing yourself to do something but will, in fact, be enjoying whatever it is you are doing.

You will be driven by an incredible power. All you have to do is steer and enjoy the process. Discipline, then, does not mean taking the time to do an unpleasant task. It means taking the time to examine and confirm your motives so that the task becomes pleasant. It is a totally internal process, not an external process. And if you can't find the motive, DON'T DO IT because it is probably the wrong thing for you to do.

Now let's relate this process to personal finance.

One of the toughest things to do is save money from your paycheck. There are always other pressing priorities that need to be taken care of. And, as we have previously discussed, expenses somehow seem to expand with incomes, so there is seldom any money left over.

The solution is to develop a good enough reason why you want to save your money and not spend it. If you do, you will regard your savings as if it was just another bill, and you will PAY YOURSELF FIRST, and place those funds into savings before you take care of any other bills. It's just a matter of rearranging your priorities in the order of the strength of your motivations.

And as for your debts, if you don't keep incurring new ones, the old ones will eventually get paid off.

That's how simple discipline becomes when you put it in it's proper perspective.

And if you apply this principle to anything you really want to accomplish, if it's "happenable", it will happen.

Capital is saved from profits.

DAVID RICARDO, 1817

Beware of little expenses. A small leak will sink a great ship.

BENJAMIN FRANKLIN, 1758

It is no secret that organized crime in America takes in over forty billion dollars a year. This is quite a profitable sum, especially when one considers that the Mafia spends very little for office supplies.

WOODY ALLEN, 1974

Only Americans have mastered the art of being prosperous though broke.

KELLY FORDYCE, 1969

CHAPTER 7

Your personal finances are your business but you have to find the profit

WHETHER WE WANT TO BELIEVE IT OR NOT, we are all in our own business.

Just like any business, whether we work for someone else, or whether we are self-employed, we have personal income coming in and we have personal expenses going out. We don't make a profit unless there is something left over between the two.

Smart businessmen know that their profits don't come from income because their income is really controlled by their competition. Profit really comes by watching expenses.

If you are a salaried employee, your boss controls your income. The only thing you have to control is your expenses.

Earning more income does not necessarily mean you will make a profit because if you spend the excess, you will be in the same boat as if you didn't get a raise. The only difference will be that you will have had more money pass through your checking account.

All you really need to do is take a look at all the multi-million dollar corporations that have gone bankrupt.

Look at Eastern Airlines. A company producing billions of dollars of cash flow, yet bankrupt. The problem wasn't that they needed more revenue. The problem was that they didn't watch their expenses.

A friend of mine, the managing partner of the local Peat Marwick office phrased it this way: "Where there is cash flow, there is a profit. It is up to you to find it."

Again, look at Robert Maxwell's empire. While he was alive, he was able to juggle the checkbooks. When he died, the house of cards collapsed on top of his family.

Personal finances are no different than business finances, yet few people recognize this simple fact.

Having spent a few years in the business of personal finance, I have had the opportunity to take a close look at many individuals who, on the surface, appeared to be quite prosperous. They were either successful business people or highly-paid corporate executives who had all the trappings that went with their positions (expensive cars, yachts, luxurious homes, club memberships, exotic vacations and so on).

They came to me because even though everything appeared grand on the outside, they felt there was a problem deep down inside.

They were right!

Once I had the opportunity to take a close look at their income and spending patterns, I could see that any slight disruption in their business or their job could bring them to the edge of bankruptcy.

Everything they owned was strictly dependent on them producing the same or higher level of income each year.

Their liquid reserves were so low, that if their personal income stopped they could not survive a year.

On the surface they may have looked just fine, but by taking a closer look, the picture appeared very different.

Let's take a look at a typical personal balance sheet of Mr. Executive who may be employed by any one of some 2,000 major companies in the U.S. Don't get thrown off if you feel the numbers are much higher than your personal situation. Just subtract a zero or multiply these same numbers by a percentage and you'll be surprised how close they might be to where you are right now.

Here is the example:

Value of Residence and Vacation Home:	$ 950,000
Mortgages:	(650,000)
Misc. Debts:	(65,000)
Qual. Plan:	120,000
Liquid Assets:	260,000
(Stocks, Bonds, Bank Accounts)	
Other Prop:	<u>300,000</u>
(Net Equity in Boat, Jewelry,	
Personal Effects, Furniture,	
Raw Land, Partnership Interests)	
Net Worth:	$ 915,000

At first glance Mr. and Mrs. Executive may look like they are in pretty good shape. They have a net worth of close to a million dollars and appear to have some liquidity.

Now let's see what else is there.

Net income after taxes and other withholdings:	$320,000
(including bonus and stock options)	
Expenses:	300,000
(including boat upkeep, college expenses and alimony)	

Still doesn't look too bad, right?

O.K. now let's take a really close look.

He is 54 years old and is a senior executive with a major corporation. She is 33 and a housewife. It is his second marriage and he has children in high school and college from his first marriage, and very high alimony and child support payments.

The company did not do so well the last couple of years and he will not get his bonus which netted him $60,000. In addition, since the company did not do so well, the stock options that he was counting on selling (he has been using his stock options to supplement his income) are not "in the money," which means there would be another net shortfall of $40,000 from his income.

That means that for next year, his expenses will be higher than his income by about $80,000.

The problem is that he can't sell his boat because due to the recession, the proceeds would be less than his debt, and the partnership interests and the jewelry are totally nonliquid.

Another problem is his company is not doing so well, and they are bringing in new blood to revitalize the business. His job could be on the line.

How long does it take to find a job grossing around $500,000 per year when you are 54 years old? Especially if the current company problems are blamed on you.

Oh, one more minor detail. The Real Estate market in the area where they have their home has been depressed, and estimates are that homes are selling at 25 percent below appraised values.

Here is the real picture. If he loses his job, based on his present spending pattern, all his liquid assets will be used up in about six months. It costs him $100,000 per year to maintain his residence and his vacation home, and it would probably cost him $250,000 to sell them because of the depressed market. It costs him $50,000 per year to maintain his boat, and it could cost him as much as $100,000 to sell it now.

The rest of his expenses include lease payments on two Mercedes' and a Jaguar, alimony/child support plus the cost of keeping his two kids in college.

How will he pay his alimony and child support? How will he keep his two kids in college? How will he live when his liquid assets run out? What kind of a job would he be able to finally get? But worst of all, since he has so few years left to retirement, wherever he goes, he won't be able to accumulate enough money in the pension plan. What happens then?

Now let's stop and think for a moment how all this might have come about.

I am sure that twenty years ago our senior executive was a middle manager somewhere, earning what in today's dollars might be $40,000 or $60,000 or perhaps even as much as $80,000 per year.

As his position improved so did his income, and naturally, he began improving his standard of living as his income grew. There is nothing wrong with that. Or is there?

Let's say this is not him then but it is you now. You've just been promoted and got yourself a hefty pay raise. The recent increase in real estate prices in your area has built up the equity in your home.

You think it will be nice to move uptown and mingle with new neighbors who always appeared to be one step higher on the economic ladder than you. Social opportunities in the new neighborhood aren't available in your present community. Also, the new home is so much bigger and roomier and brighter than the old one.

So you put a pencil to the whole transaction and it looks like a cinch. The equity in your present home will mean a sizeable down payment toward the new house. And although the new mortgage may be triple the old one, it falls within your income range, based on the extra income your raise will bring.

You are ready to go for it but is there anything you may have overlooked? Now let's figure out all the fringes and peripherals that go with this new house and see how they may stack up in your budget.

Consider this: now that you are moving into a new home, would the old furniture do or would you want to decorate the new home like you have always wanted to?

Since you now have plenty of back yard, why not build a swimming pool? And while you are remodeling, why not change a few odds and ends and throw it all in the mortgage?

Once you move in, you now have to live the part. You can't put the old cars in the garage. What will your new neighbors think? You need to impress them that you are at least as good as they are.

Why not use some of the equity of the old house and trade your old cars in for a couple of new foreign ones. And not necessarily Hondas or Toyotas.

Naturally, both you and your spouse will have to have a cellular phone in the car since no one in the neighborhood is without one.

The whole neighborhood will also be watching for the kind of car you will buy your kids on their sixteenth birthdays.

No more bargain basement clothes either. You'll need a new wardrobe for the family, one commensurate with your new lifestyle.

And since you now have such a beautiful home, you'll have to entertain right, especially if you plan to invite the neighbors. A few microwave snacks and drinks won't do anymore. Your parties will now have to be catered, including at least one bartender and a couple of waiters.

When vacation time rolls around you just can't pile the family in the old RV anymore. Europe or the Caribbean are the de rigueur, but the Far East would really be impresive, filling your Kodak carousel with slides and your living room with friends and neighbors dying to hear about your adventures.

The costs of moving up are high indeed. They increase geometrically.

But let's suppose that Mr. Executive did not fall into the trap of trying to maintain his standard of living to be commensurate with his income and his position. Let's say he had the presence of mind to hold back and save half of all the raises he had ever gotten from the time his income went from $60,000 per year to his present compensation package of approximately $500,000 over this twenty year period.

By now, his investments would have been well into a couple of million dollars, and he probably would have been enjoying his house with a very low mortgage.

His boat and his cars would probably not have been financed and they too would have been free and clear.

To illustrate this point, let's now take a look at our Mr. Executive. Perhaps 10 years earlier, and what his situation might have looked like had he done things a little differently while he was a middle manager with that same company.

Here is our Mr. Executive, age 44, earning $120,000 annually from his job while his wife is pulling $40,000 per year from a family owned retail business. (All this income is in today's dollars.) Even though she draws a full salary, in reality she only spends an average of 10 hours per week in running the business because they have a full-time manager in charge. The rest of the time she spends in running the household and taking care of their two children.

They also own two small apartment buildings, one with two rental units and the other with three rental units, both of which include commercial spaces and the combined value of the real estate is approximately $500,000. They collect a gross rent of $50,000 annually, most of which goes to pay the mortgages and the expenses on the building.

Here is their financial statement:

Assets:

Residence	$ 250,000	
Summer Home	100,000	
Rental Property	500,000	
Value of Business	120,000	
401K	80,000	
I.R.A.	60,000	
Liquid Assets (Stocks/Bonds Etc)	140,000	
Personal Effects & Autos	50,000	
	$1,300,000	$1,300,000

Liabilities:

Home Mortgage	$ 20,000	
(3 yrs left of a 15 yr mortgage)		
Summer Home Mortgage	50,000	
(5 yrs left of a 15 yr mortgage)		
Mortgages on Rental Property	250,000	
(8 yrs left of a 15 yr mortgage)		
Misc Debts	20,000	
	$ 340,000	340,000
Net Worth		$ 960,000

Mr. and Mrs. Executive live on about $90,000 net per year, which leaves them about $25,000 annually for savings after they pay their taxes and withholdings. They drive a Jeep and a Honda.

You will notice that our 54-year-old top executive's net worth is about the same as the net worth of our 44-year-old manager.

The main difference is that the 44-year-old manager, by doing things just a little differently is within a few years of achieving his financial independence. Within 8 years, all the mortgages he has will be paid off and between the income on his rental property and the income from the retail business, they will be able to live very well whether he kept his job or not.

On the other hand, our 54-year-old executive, who has been spending his salary as he went along, is not even close to achieving financial independence, even though his earned income is four times greater and his net worth is about the same.

The difference between the two has been essentially that our younger executive saved a greater proportion of his income by keeping his living expenses down, which he reinvested in areas that included "man at work" and "money at work", -that is Real Estate and Closely Held Business (which we will be discussing in more detail in the next chapter).

By doing this, his net worth is increasing by leaps and bounds because he has high mortgage paydown, along with capital appreciation of investments plus the savings he realizes from earned income.

By the time our 44-years-old executive reaches age 54 and earns a half million dollar per year income from his job, his net worth will be several million dollars. By that time, if he chose to spend his whole salary to indulge himself, he could do so because he will no longer be dependent on earned income.

But let's not stop there. Let's go back another twelve years to where our Mr. Executive was still a middle manager, perhaps earning $50,000 annually and his wife was a teacher, adding another $20,000 per year to their income.

He is now 32 years old. He just bought a home for $90,000 which has an $80,000 15-year mortgage. His savings in his I.R.A. and 401K total $24,000. And that's all he has. That means that during the next twelve years, by buying income real estate and a closely held business, taking short mortgages and making sure he spent less than what he earned, his net worth grew to close to $1 million.

And that in a nutshell is why living up to your income is just not good business! To survive in future years, you need a hefty profit between your income and your expenses.

But most important of all, that profit needs to stay in your bank account and not somebody else's.

The only good budget is a balanced budget.

ADAM SMITH, 1776

*Failure is more frequently from want of energy
than from want of capital.*

DANIEL WEBSTER, 1838

*Capital is that part of wealth which is devoted
to obtaining further wealth.*

ALFRED MARSHALL, 1890

*The thing that I should wish to obtain from money
would be leisure with security.*

BERTRAND RUSSELL, 1935

*Economy is the science of avoiding
unnecessary expenditure, or the art of
managing our property with moderation.*

SENECA, c A.D. 40

CHAPTER 8

Transition from "man at work" to "capital at work"

AS WE HAVE SEEN IN THE LAST CHAPTER, had our Mr. Executive created enough capital during his most productive years, he would not have had to worry about keeping his job or providing for his retirement. He had plenty of opportunities to do so, even without seriously affecting his standard of living, yet he insisted on regarding his income as his source of wealth and forgot to take the necessary steps to prevent a possible financial disaster.

The last chapter emphasizes the importance of creating capital during your most productive years in order to take care of those years that may not be so productive.

You will also notice that our Mr. Executive had almost a million dollar net worth, yet that still didn't take care of him.

The name of the game is to have enough capital to take care of you in proportion to your spending habits. This is what I call the "Financial Independence Factor," but I will talk about this in another chapter.

Let's talk about creating capital. If I get a little too simplistic for you in the next few paragraphs, please bear with me. In order to see the big picture, you sometimes have to break things down to their most common denominator.

There are only three ways that you can create capital. You can convert income to capital. You can start or invent something that others would be willing to exchange their capital for. Or you can trade some of your capital for something and then improve it so someone else would be willing to give you more than what you had paid for it. In most instances, what you are really doing is converting labor to capital. Whether that labor is physical or intellectual, doesn't really matter. Your productivity within this process is everything.

No matter what the basic source of the capital happens to be, this capital will be throwing off some kind of income if you put it to work. But it is up to you to make it work, because without your effort, some forms of capital will never throw off an income.

That means that there are really only two sources of income:

MAN AT WORK and CAPITAL AT WORK

Or some combination of both.

Most of us depend on only one source of income, that is "man at work." Very seldom do we concentrate on having the other one going for us, that is "capital at work."

We spend all our energies chasing higher salaries. Yet it is so much easier, simpler and more productive to chase after capital and let it first enhance our earned incomes and improve our standard of living, and eventually provide the income we need to live without having to depend on our "man at work" capacity.

The most obvious and the simplest form of creating capital is by converting earned income to capital. That is, good old savings.

Most people think that savings come from "Marginal Income".

By definition, marginal income is that amount of money that is left over after paying all the bills. In practice, "marginal income" is a phantom. It doesn't exist! Because in most instances, when you get your paycheck and start paying your bills, in the end it is not income that you have left over, but more bills.

And this holds true, in most instances, regardless of how high or how low your earned income happens to be.

I have personally seen this phenomena at work with just about everybody including businessmen, professionals, executives, and especially sports figures and entertainers.

In the first chapter we touched on the fact that expenses will somehow magically expand with income. Partially this is due to external forces such as inflation and taxes (about which we will be talking in a later chapter). By and large, however, it is our own internal forces that drive our spending patterns spiraling upward, and those forces are mostly driven by our egos.

The problem is that it is very difficult to control our egos.

Let's take a few minutes to examine this "ego" question in some depth, and as we do, gain some insight into why the Duckworths went bankrupt.

Controlling our egos can be very easy if we study a little Mazlow, the famous behavioral sciences guru.

The event that made Dr. Mazlow famous was his theory on the Hierarchy of Needs.

In summary, the theory goes something like this:

All of us have certain needs programmed into our psyche which drive our behavior. Those needs follow a certain hierarchy, meaning that a specific set of needs does not begin to manifest itself until the current set is satisfied. There are five such layers of needs and the first three layers can be satisfied while the fourth and the fifth are insatiable.

The first layer of needs are Physiological. This refers to our need to have our stomachs full, a roof over our head and a sex partner to play with. Once this set of needs is satisfied, the Security needs click in. That is the need for those physiological needs to keep being satisfied in the future. Once we feel relatively secure that these needs will be met regularly in the foreseeable future, our Social needs begin to emerge. This refers to our need to interact with other human beings. As soon as we have satisfactory relationships with other people, our Ego needs, which are insatiable, begin to show their ugly head. That is where our problems of over-spending begin and, if handled effectively, may end. The fifth and final set of needs are Self Actualization, the search for how we, as individual human beings, may relate to the rest of the universe and what our role in this scenario may be and the need to, in some way, contribute to hummanity. These too, are insatiable.

But let's get back to our ego needs. The interesting point is that the ego needs, beside standing on their own by having us strive to "become number one," " become a winner," "be recognized for our accomplishments," or just plain break our back so that we can hang another lousy plaque on the wall, are very closely related to our social needs.

For example, we believe that if we have a big house, drive a Mercedes, own a big yacht, or just plain throw a lot of money around, a lot of people will want to become our friends. Conversely, if we already have a lot of friends, our ego is fed by having more and bigger and better things than our friends. So we spend more money to have more friends and then we spend even more money to impress our friends.

This is similar to the cat chasing its tail or the shark eating its own flesh. In other words, a feeding frenzy, and an insatiable one to boot.

If we have zillions of loose cash to do this with, it probably is okay. It makes us feel good and that is all that really counts.

However, if we do this while we still have to work for a living and don't have millions to maintain our living standard forever, we are on a treadmill that will eventually destroy us. Especially if we have plenty of income, yet we have to borrow in order to indulge our over-spending.

Most of us who are on this treadmill are on it only because we don't understand the dynamics of the force that is driving us. We think that we are responding to a undeniable "need" when we borrow ourselves into oblivion to buy a more expensive car, house or boat.

We kid ourselves by saying that we are doing it for our families and our children, while in reality, we do it for no other reason than to satisfy a primary need that has been programmed into us.

If we understand this urge for what it is, just like we understand the urge for sex or for gluttony, we can control it and laugh it away. However, if we allow it to consume us, it will destroy our lives.

Just think of it this way: If we feel the urge to have sex, do we respond to this urge by raping the first person we run into for whom we might feel a physical attraction?

No, we are too civilized for rape!

Then why do we insist on raping our present savings and future income if we feel the urge for our friends to see us in a new Mercedes?

So, if we think about Mazlow the next time we see a snazzy car and begin to picture ourselves behind the wheel, chances are we will have won over our egos.

Keeping Mazlow in mind, let's now see how we might take the first steps in creating some capital.

There are really only three ways to convert earned income to capital:

1. Save from current income
2. Pay down principal of debts created for capital purchases.
3. Reinvest earnings on invested capital.

Every one of those methods is in direct conflict with our egos.

Here are some examples that illustrate this conflict:

Why should we save if we need a bigger house? (Remember the word "need.")

We can enjoy a bigger and more expensive house if we take a thirty- year mortgage on it, instead of a fifteen-year mortgage on the other cheaper house.

Why should we take a fifteen-year smaller mortgage, when we can take a thirty-year bigger mortgage? Isn't mortgage interest one of the few tax deductions left? (Nobody is in a 100 percent tax bracket. Two-thirds of the mortgage interest payment is your money that could be going toward savings instead of toward the banks profit.)

Why should we reinvest the interest and the dividends when we could use this money to enjoy a Mercedes instead of having to drive a Volvo?

After all, what is money good for except to enjoy it? We may as well spend it while we are young and can enjoy it, instead of waiting and maybe never getting to see it because we will be too old to enjoy it or we will be dead.

These are powerful arguments in favor of giving in to our egos. The point to keep in mind is that the name of the game is to have our capital provide us with enough income from "capital at work" so we can eventually do all the things we really want to do. But if we use our earned incomes to give in to our momentary ego needs or if we use income from capital for the same purpose before we have enough capital accumulated, we will always remain slaves to "man at work."

Now let's talk about the tricks we can play with ourselves in order to maximize converting our earned income to capital:

1. Place the maximum into your company 401k plan. If you are self-employed, start your own Qualified plan.

2. If the company you work for is solid financially and they have a Non-Qualified Deferred Compensation Plan, place the maximum in it.

3. Pre-pay home and other real estate mortgage payments. That is probably your best investment.

4. Pay yourself first into a regular savings account before you pay any bills.

Most people have a tough time living on a budget, so you are in good company. However, if you have put the money away first and saved it, chances are you are not going to spend it.

Target your expenses and separate them in three categories:

1. Regular monthly expenses. These are your mortgage and car payments, food, etc.

2. Periodic Expenses. These include clothing, vacations, home repairs etc.

3. Savings. This is where you place the first check.

Use two checking accounts and a money market account to handle the cash flow. If you follow this system, you'd be surprised how much you would be able to save. (See Figure #1)

Here are some of what I call "Words of Financial Wisdom" that you might want to be thinking about when your ego begins to show its ugly head while you are following the system:

- It's not how much you earn, it's how much you keep.
- It's not the size of your net worth, it's how long your net worth will last if your income stopped.
- It's not how much you earn on your investments, it's how much your net worth increases by each year.
- It's not the size of your tax deduction, it's what you have to spend to get it. Nobody is in a 100 percent tax bracket.
- It's not how much you own, it's how little you owe.
- It's not how well you live, it's how much you have to spend to live this way.
- It's not how hard you work, it's how you work.
- It's not how much you earn, it's how much you depend on your earnings.
- It's not what you earn on your investments, it's what you have left over after taxes and inflation.
- It's not what you have, it's what you do with what you have.
- It's not what your neighbor has, it's what you really want to have.
- It's not how much leverage you use, it's the reason you use it.
- It's not how much you earn, it's how much you spend.
- It's not the quantity of assets you have to retire on, it's how many years you have to live on those assets and what inflation will do to them during this time.

- It's not how much assets you die with, it's how you enjoy those assets while you are living.
- It's not what you have, it's what you want.

Keep these "Words of Financial Wisdom" on your mind whenever you are making any spending decisions, and you'll be surprised how much less you will spend.

It is easier to make money than to save it;
one is exertion, the other self-denial.

THOMAS C. HALIBURTON, 1853

CONTROLLING DISBURSEMENTS

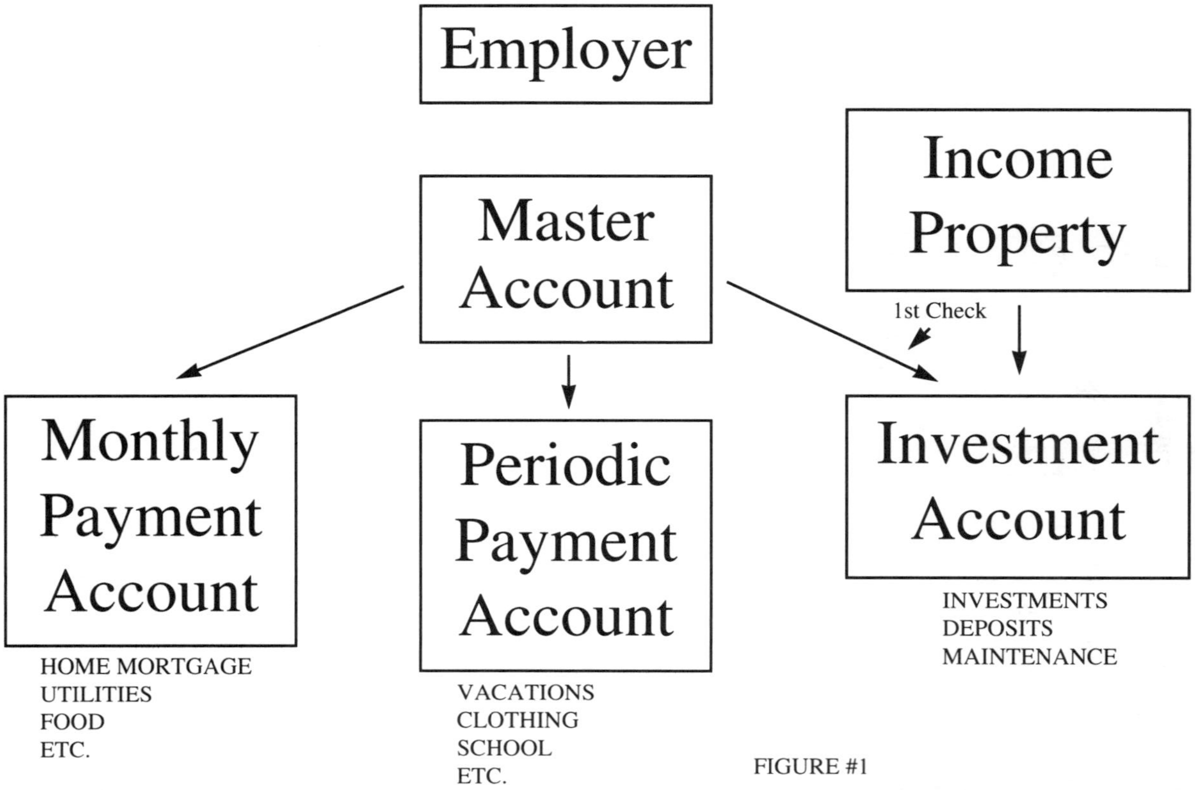

Employer

Income Property

Master Account

1st Check → Investment Account

INVESTMENTS
DEPOSITS
MAINTENANCE

Periodic Payment Account

VACATIONS
CLOTHING
SCHOOL
ETC.

Monthly Payment Account

HOME MORTGAGE
UTILITIES
FOOD
ETC.

FIGURE #1

He who has money has in his pocket those who have none.

LYOF N. TOLSTOY, 1895

There are two times in a man's life when he should not speculate:
when he can't afford it, and when he can.

MARK TWAIN, 1894

Almost any man knows how to earn money, but not
one in a million knows how to spend it.

HENRY DAVID THOREAU, 1854

*The entire essence of America
is the hope to first make money
then make money with money -
then make lots of money
with lots of money.*

PAUL ERDMAN, 1967

Forget "return on investment," it won't make you rich, but "wealth factor" will!

THE POINT WHERE WE HAVE REACHED financial independence is the point where we no longer have to depend on "man at work" to continue our standard of living, but where "capital at work" would do the job indefinitely.

The two most important factors that go into this calculation are really the amount of capital one has and the amount of income required to maintain a certain standard of living.

To be sure, there are other factors also, like inflation, the rate of return on investments, and how many years you still have to live, along with any additional capital or income that may come along the way.

But the bottom line is: "How much are you spending?" and "How much do you have?"

If you were to pick one factor as the most important, that would definitely be: "How much are you spending?"

Let's compare the street person who has an almost zero spending habit and no capital, to Robert Maxwell who, based on news media reports, had an insatiable spending habit with a huge amount of capital which he was consuming to feed his spending habit.

In this case, the street person may have had a greater degree of financial independence than Robert Maxwell, because he may survive longer without having to earn an income. The point here is not that being a street person may be more preferable to the other alternative, but that huge apparent wealth does not necessarily guarantee "Financial Independence," and that lack of wealth is also not a deciding factor. Each individual has to make the decision where in this spectrum he or she may feel most comfortable.

So, with the above thought in mind, let's examine the role that what I call the "Wealth Factor" and the "Financial Independence Factor" will play in helping you become "rich."

Many times we kid ourselves when we look at the investment performance of our portfolio.

If it looks like we have had another double-digit year, we think we are right on track for reaching our financial objectives.

The problem is that the investment results we bring in through the front door may be going out the back door in unnecessary and controllable expenses.

What good is it to take the risks necessary to make 18 percent on your money if you reinvested all those profits with your Mercedes garage mechanic?

To keep track of how you are really doing you need to keep your eye on more than just how much money your financial assets are earning.

The elements that make for a real increase in your net worth are: your income, your expenses, your taxes, inflation rate, the capital gain (or loss) on your assets, return on your investments, your debt paydown and your savings.

No one element is most important. The name of the game is to make sure that each year your net worth is higher than the year before after you have adjusted all your assets for inflation that year.

For example, let's say you own $300,000 in real estate the value of which increased by 3 percent last year. Your mortgage paydown was $12,000, the $100,000 that you keep in the savings account paid you a paltry 5 percent interest, and you managed to save $10,000 from your income. That means that your net worth increased by $36,000 representing 9 percent of your assets.

If inflation ran at 6 percent, that means that you were ahead of the game by 3 percent or $12,000 which is not bad.

But let's suppose that instead of carrying a 15-year mortgage on your house, you opted for a 30-year mortgage and, as a result, your mortgage paydown was only $3000 instead of $12,000. And instead of saving $10,000 you spent $5,000 more than you earned. However, your stockbroker was a real wizard and earned you $16,000 on your investments instead of the 5 percent the bank was paying you.

Even though you really did well on your investments, your net worth increased only by $23,000. Since inflation took away $24,000 of your assets, that year, you really went backward by $1,000 on your net worth even though you did very well on your investments that year.

Where should you put your emphasis if you want to get rich? Obviously it shouldn't be on your investments, unless you have no earned income, no debts and no other appreciable assets.

Unfortunately, most people focus on the return on their investments as a measure of their progress, and forget about the fact that other factors are much more important than an extra couple of percentage points you can make on those investments.

Is it worth those extra couple of percentage points, to greatly increase the risk to your capital?

It's tough enough to accumulate it, so why take unnecessary risks for such a small payoff?

For the above reasons, you should use only the "Wealth Factor" as a measure of your progress. This way you will not be kidding yourself and will know exactly whether you took a step foreward or backward in your net worth.

Here are the elements that go into your "Wealth Factor" calculation: (See Figure #2)

- After-tax return on investment
- Debt paydown
- Capital appreciation
- Inflation
- Net capital (Net Worth)
- Current savings

Now that you know how to monitor your "wealth factor", here are some steps you can take in monitoring your progress toward financial independence.

The idea is to reach a point where "capital at work" will maintain the same standard of living as "man at work."

At first, you will be able to achieve this for a limited period of time. As you progress, the length of time that you can go without earning an income should increase. Eventually, you should reach a point where your capital would be able to maintain you indefinitely.

Here is how you do it:

First you target your expenses needed to maintain your present standard of living.

Then you target a capital base that you will need to maintain this standard for a fixed period of time. At first a year, then two or three years and then longer.

Once you reach your goal, then you can begin expanding your living standard along with increasing the length of time that you can maintain it.

The factors that go into calculating this "Financial Independence" factor are:

- Future Expenses
- Inflation
- Rate of return on investment
- Taxes
- Life expectancy
- Future Capital creation opportunities
- Future Windfall income opportunities.

The "Financial Independence" factor represents the percentage of your remaining life that can be spent without earning an income and strictly relying on "capital at work" to see you through.

Therefore if you take:

The number of years capital will last after deducting annual living expenses, adjusting them for inflation, and adding an after tax return on the remaining capital and dividing this figure by the number of years of your life expectancy, you will then have your "Financial Independence" factor.

The closer the factor is to one, the closer you are to your goal. (See Figure #3)

The problem is that as your capital and earned income grows, so does your desire to spend it. That is when your attitude, your values, and your control over your ego must come together to overcome these pressures.

The most important thing to keep in mind is that the road to financial independence really does not represent sacrifice or denial. On the contrary, eventually it really represents a better standard of living then you could possibly imagine because you will have both "capital at work" and "man at work" providing you with the material things you always wanted.

And all this without the ulcers!

CALCULATING "WEALTH FACTOR"

"Wealth Factor" represents the percentage by which your net worth has increased during the last 12 months.

R - Return on Investment (After Tax)
D - Debt Paydown on Capital
A - Capital Appreciation
I - Inflation
C - Net Capital (Net Worth)
S - Current Savings

$$\frac{(R + D + A + S) - I}{C} = \text{Wealth Factor}$$

Return on investment is only a small piece of the measuring rod used to determine whether you are progressing toward Financial Independence.

FIGURE #2

CALCULATING "FINANCIAL INDEPENDENCE FACTOR"

"Financial Independence Factor" represents the percentage of your remaining life that can be spent without earning an income. Strictly depending on Money at Work and not on Man at Work.

N - Number of Years Capital Will Last After Deducting Annual Expenses, Adjusting Them for an Assumed Inflation Rate Each Year and Adding an After-Tax Return on Investment on the Remaining Capital

L - Number of Years Left to Life Expectancy Plus 5

$$\frac{N}{L} = \text{Financial Independence Factor}$$

The higher the percentage, the closer you are to "Total' Financial Independence. The problem is as your capital (and income) grows, so does your desire to spend.

That's where it is most important for you to control your living standard and not allow your neighbors to do it for you.

FIGURE #3

If you would know the value of money, go and try to borrow some.

BENJAMIN FRANKLIN, 1757

Credit buying is much like being drunk. The buzz happens immediately, and it gives you a lift... The hangover comes the day after.

JOYCE BROTHERS, 1971

A banker is a fellow who lends his umbrella when the sun is shining and wants it back the minute it begins to rain.

MARK TWAIN, 1893

Do not accustom yourself to consider debt only as an inconvenience. You will find it a calamity.

SAMUEL JOHNSON, 1758

It's not politics that is worrying this Country; it's the Second Payment.

WILL ROGERS, 1927

CHAPTER 10

The road to the poorhouse is paved with "leverage"

EVERY ONCE IN A WHILE, you might hear the following advice from your friendly stockbroker: "Smart people know how to use leverage. You have a lot of equity in both your stock and bond portfolio and your house. That equity is just sitting there and not doing anything. Let's put it to work and margin your portfolio and take a mortgage on your house, and we will be able to triple your investments."

If you hear those words, run in the other direction.

Sometimes it does make financial sense to borrow against one piece of capital in order to invest in another piece of capital that you might have reason to believe would appreciate in value faster or have an income greater than the cost of your borrowing. An example of this might be to borrow against a piece of income real estate that you own in order to purchase another piece of income real estate or to buy into a closely held business that you might control.

But to indiscriminately borrow against your portfolio or your home in order to speculate in some financial product such as common stocks or limited partnership shares, is at best very questionable and risky but more than likely just plain foolish. The end result will be in most instances the conversion of your liquid assets into brokerage commissions.

To my way of thinking, borrowing by using present capital as collateral to speculate on some financial asset is nothing more than just plain incurring more debt.

And debt is a real killer.

Most people confuse debt with leverage because there is sometime a very fine line between the two. The best way to avoid this pitfall is to remember that you should only borrow against capital whenever there is an element of "man at work" related to the new investment. This way you have some control over the investment results.

However, if you have no control over investment results, that is if you have borrowed to place your money into "passive investments" you have incurred debt in order to speculate and have not used "leverage" in it's proper sense.

But the worst type of debt is when one borrows to finance their standard of living, or consumer debt as it is sometimes called.

What most people don't realize is that this type of loan places a mortgage on your future earnings. In addition, it actually reduces your future standard of living, because a portion of what you earn from that point on is used to pay for something that you have already used and the interest you pay on that loan, makes that used item that much more expensive.

As one of our founding fathers so aptly phrased it:

The principle of spending money to be paid by posterity, under the name of funding, is but swindling futurity on a large scale.

THOMAS JEFFERSON, 1789

That means that your future income no longer belongs to you but to the lending company. And that also means that you must keep earning that income until your loan is paid off.

In other words, consumer debt makes you a slave to your earned income and, in fact, to your job.

Ralph Waldo Emerson said it this way:

A man in debt is so far a slave.

When I was running my insurance and securities operations, the people I recruited were salespeople who, by their nature, had huge egos. The greater the ego, the more effective the salesperson and the more money he or she would be making for me. In those days, I am not so proud to say, I used this ego weakness to my advantage. I would encourage my salespeople to take out large loans, purchase big homes and fancy cars. I would sometimes even lend them the money to do this. I would tell them that in order for them to be effective in getting more and bigger customers, they had to look and act "successful." It wasn't very difficult for me to convince them of this because this was what they wanted to believe.

My reward was that they had to work twice as hard to pay off all those debts, generating a lot of commissions and overrides for me. Their egos drove them deeper and deeper into debt and they, in fact, became slaves to their jobs.

Even though I felt uncomfortable doing this, at the time I didn't feel guilty because this method was the "modus operandi" which the insurance companies and the brokerage houses considered "proper and effective management." Now that I am out of the business, and have an opportunity to objectively reflect on this practice, I am not proud of what I did. I feel this was a destructive form of manipulation of human beings. Life had to butt up against me before I saw this clearly.

Some people seem to be proud of their debts as if to say that by having a large debt structure, one is somehow more worthy a person than one who may not have the same borrowing capacity. They sometimes call themselves "highly leveraged".

Don't believe it. Leverage, as I have discussed, when used wisely, is a money earner. Debt, on the other hand, can be a noose around your neck and is definitely bad for your health.

It can keep you awake at night, give you ulcers and high blood pressure, cause heart attacks, and be responsible for a multitude of stress-related diseases that will generally make your life miserable.

The first rule of thumb to follow if you want to sleep nights, is to avoid borrowing to finance your standard of living.

This means avoiding credit card loans, auto loans, and other consumer loans.

This type of borrowing is very expensive and it increases your costs of purchases and, as we discussed before, actually reduces your future standard of living.

The real problem is chances are your income will never increase at a high enough rate to compensate for taxes and inflation, let alone the additional costs related to paying off your debts. And this is how, even though our incomes double and triple within a few short years, we keep sinking deeper and deeper into the hole.

The best solution, of course, is to pay for all consumable items in cash. Do without until you have the money to pay for them.

Have you noticed how immigrants, who come to this country with just the shirt on their backs, within a few short years accumulate real wealth in real estate, business ownership and eventually financial assets. "How do they do it?" you probably ask yourself.

Well, I believe that one of the reasons is that in the beginning, credit is not very readily available to immigrants, so that they get used to paying cash for everything and doing without until they have the money.

I believe there is a lesson to be learned in this.

Somehow, many of us seem to be programmed with a viewpoint that if we want something, it is okay to get it now and pay for it later.

This attitude transcends itself not only for material things but for most things we want in life. As an extension of this attitude, whenever we make a mistake, we do everything we can to avoid paying for this mistake.

Life becomes so much simpler if we pay for what we want before we get it and if we make a mistake, pay the price for the mistake and go on with our life.

The problem is that most of us don't follow this "natural order", and waste much of our energies trying to avoid paying for our mistakes while paying through the nose for the things we put on "the easy payment plan."

However, if we follow the "natural order" of things we will be so much happier and much more productive. We have to learn to "Pay the price for what we want first, so that we can really enjoy it! If we make a mistake in our life, pay the price quickly - get it over with - and go on with enjoying our life!"

But if we must have something now before we paid for it, here are some simple rules to follow:

- Pay credit card balances in full when you get the bill. If you can't do that, don't buy the stuff.
- Take short term loans on cars equal to three years or less. If you lease, take zero residual value and make sure your lease is for no longer than three years. If you can't do that, buy a cheaper car.
- Remember, to only spend your present income. Not your future

income. If you start mortgaging tomorrow's earnings, you will always be playing catch-up.

• Take short term mortgages on your home and other real estate properties. No more than 15 years. If you can't afford the extra payments, buy a cheaper house. Or in case of income property, if a fifteen-year mortgage will not give you positive cash flow within a reasonable period of time, perhaps you are paying too much for the property.

Most people wind up taking 30-year mortgages because that is what the banks usually prefer the public to accept. This is the most profitable mortgage for the bank. A shorter mortgage, on the other hand, reduces the amount of interest due on the loan, and boosts the amount of principal paid down in the early years. Banks don't like this.

Here are some examples:

If you take out a $100,000 mortgage at a 10 percent interest rate, you will pay $215,926. in interest during the 30-year term of the loan.

However, if you take out a 15-year mortgage, your total interest payments will be $93,429—-a $122,427 savings.

If you currently have a 30-year mortgage, you can achieve the same result by simply paying an extra 20 percent of your mortgage payment toward principal. That means that the difference between a 30-year mortgage and a 15-year mortgage is only 20 percent.

You might then say to yourself: I'll take out a 30-year mortgage and pay the extra 20 percent and pay it off in 15 years.

Don't kid yourself. Somehow, when it comes for you to make that extra prepayment, you will always have something better to spend your money on. If you commit yourself to the 15-year loan, you will have a forced savings going for you.

If you now have a 30-year mortgage and decide to start prepaying it, you should check out the terms of your mortgage agreement. Many lending institutions include a prepayment penalty clause, the purpose of which is to discourage you from prepaying.

At the time you make your mortgage, you have some leverage. Banks love to include prepayment penalties in the agreement. However, if you tell them you will not take the mortgage if they include this penalty, in most instances they will remove this clause.

The other thing to watch in the mortgage is the paydown of

principal in the early years. Most people will either refinance or sell their home within five to ten years. That is all the more reason why you should take out a short mortgage.

On a $100,000/30-year mortgage, the principal paid down during the first five years is $3,428. In ten years it is $9,862. That means that in a ten-year period you will have paid down less than 10 percent of the principal. It would take you 24 years to pay down 50 percent of the mortgage.

On a 15-year mortgage, however, the principal paid in the first five years is $18,683 and within ten years you will have paid down 50 percent of the loan. That means that your principal paydown is almost five times faster on a 15-year mortgage than on a 30-year mortgage. That means that if you plan to sell your property within five or ten years, you will have much more equity with a 15-year loan.

For banks, long mortgages are where the profits are. But for you, the homeowner, you make your money on equity and that is why you should never take a long mortgage.

In summary, if you must borrow, do it to make a capital investment that includes "man at work" as part of the profit. If you don't follow this rule, chances are you will be juggling your checkbook right up to the day of your funeral.

Debt is the slavery of the free.

PUBLILIUS SYRUS, FIRST CENTURY B.C.

In investing money, the amount of interest you want should depend on whether you want to eat well or sleep well.

J. KENFIELD MORLEY, 1937

The safest way to double your money is to fold it over once and put it in your pocket.

FRANK MCKINNEY HUBBARD, 1907

All men's gains are the fruit of venturing.

HERODOTUS, FIFTH CENTURY B.C.

Buy cheap, sell dear.

THOMAS LODGE, 1595

CHAPTER 11

Everything you ever needed to know about investing but were never told

BEFORE ANYONE STARTS PLACING their hard-earned dollars into passive investments, or "securities" if you will, one should make sure that the most important investment areas are taken care of first.

But for a couple of exceptions, I will not attempt to explore the intricate details of many types of investments available to the public in this chapter. However I will instead try to discuss the underlying philosophy behind investment, at least as I have applied it in my own situation and with my clients. You will not get any specific "stock tips" here or sophisticated approaches to real estate investment, or what the "hot" mutual funds of the day happen to be, but you should gain a fundamental knowledge of how to allocate your investment dollars so that you will have a fighting chance of hanging on to them.

Invest in Yourself:

The first place to invest should always be in yourself and your family. This is the area where one has the most amount of control over the end result and where benefits can be measured not just in dollars and cents, but in feelings of satisfaction, pride, accomplishment and peace of mind.

Invariably, those are the investments that will carry the highest return.

For example, before any money is given to a stockbroker to buy securities, the following areas should be explored and taken care of first:

- Purchase of a home
- Education for yourself and your family
- Enough money in bank accounts and/or money market funds to carry you for at least one year.
- Purchase of income property that will be managed personally.
- Investment in closely held business where you would take control and have active management participation.
- Enough life insurance, health insurance, disability insurance and property and liability insurance to take care of and protect you against various hazards.
- Once you have explored and/or taken care of all of the above investment priorities, only then should you consider some kind of passive investment such as securities.

You will note that I recommend that you should first own both an interest in a closely held business and income Real Estate property before you venture into securities. Both of those investments represent an inflation adjusted stream of income which you will never achieve with any securities and which are a key factor in your achieving financial independence. And both of those investments combine your personal ingenuity with your dollars which means that your risk/reward ratio is greatly enhanced. Now, once you have enough financial assets to maintain your lifestyle without earning an income, you really don't need those two investment sources any longer. But as long as you still need to work to pay your bills, you should not place any of your investment dollars into securities other than bonds. If you do, you are taking on too much risk with too little reward.

This is a philosophy you will never see in other books on personal finance because many people who write those books make their living with securities either directly or indirectly.

You Cannot Avoid Risk:

The most important thing to keep in mind is that there is no such thing as an investment without risk. All investments have risk.

Therefore, before you make the investment, you should be sure that you know what the risks are and how much you can stand to gain by assuming that risk.

Let's now try to break risk down to its most common denominator.

There is only one of two things that you can do with your money: You can either own something or you can loan your money to someone else. There is no other variation of investment. That is it!

The big questions then become: "How much are you going to either lend, or spend on purchasing? Who are you going lend your money to? What are you going to purchase?"

Regardless of whether you lend your money or you buy something, each one of those alternatives carry their own brand of risks and rewards.

If you decide to own something, your risks are generally related to market fluctuations, business downturns, bankruptcies, and obsolescence of the particular item that you bought.

Your rewards associated with owning something usually represent your maintaining value in the face of inflation, and that your return will be commensurate with the productivity of the particular item that you bought.

To understand this point a little bit better, let's say you decided to "own" a share of common stock. If you bought this stock when the demand for either this stock or stocks in general was low, and you held it until the demand reappeared, then you would have made a profit. If you would have done the reverse- that is, purchased the stock when the demand was high and sold it when the demand was low- you would have lost money. However, if the company went bankrupt because of poor management in the meantime, no matter how much demand there was for that type of stock, you would have lost your money. On the other hand, no matter how good the management was, and the item that they were producing suddenly was no longer used by the public (like buggies pulled by horses) you would still lose your money no matter how much demand there was for stock in general at that particular point in time. However, if you happened to have picked a company that was well managed and the product that they were producing was in demand, but we suddenly had a round of high inflation, chances are that the purchasing power of the value of the stock would have been sustained.

Sounds complicated? You bet! But this is only the beginning.

Now let's say you decided to lend someone some of your money. The rewards here are that your principal and your interest payment on that principal would be guaranteed. That means your principal and interest are fixed.

The risks are that if the person you lent the money to went bankrupt, you would lose your money. If the inflation rate was higher than the interest that you were receiving, then the purchasing power of your principal would decrease and you would have lost money. And if interest rates in general increased and you wanted to sell this loan you made because you needed the cash for something else, you would get less than your principal because it's value is commensurate with the income stream that you would receive. This means that a "loan" type investment has business risk, inflation risk and interest rate risk.

Let me give an example of this "interest rate risk" once again, because to most people who are not in the business of selling or advising on securities, it is a difficult one to understand.

Let's say that you decided to buy a U.S. Treasury 30-year bond for $1,000 and it was guaranteed to give you 8 percent interest or $80 per year. You in fact lent your money to the U.S. government.

One year later interest rates go up to 10 percent, and you need to now sell the bond because you need to fix the leak in your roof. At this point you could only get a little more than $800 for it because the income it gives is $80 per year which is 10 percent of $800. In other words you have lost $200 on an investment that was fully guaranteed by the U.S. government. Of course if you held it for another 29 years you would get the full $1000. But then you would have received a lower rate of return than what the market offered at that time for the remaining 29 years. That is "interest rate risk."

So the most important point to remember is that no matter where you place your money, it will ALWAYS be at risk. You cannot avoid risk! (See Figure #4)

You Are Always 100 Percent Invested:
What most of us don't realize is that we are always 100 percent invested at all times whether we like it or not. That means that our capital is always subject to risk.

There is no break from being invested. The only variation is the type of investment and the amount involved in each category of investment.

Even though there are only two things you can do with your money, there are five categories of investment.

The "own" type categories include "equities", "real estate" and "tangibles."

The "loan" type categories include "fixed interest investments" and "cash."

"Equities" include common stocks, including interest in your closely held business.

"Real Estate" is real estate that you own and manage personally. To my way of thinking, Real Estate Investment Trusts and Limited Partnerships are nothing more than "securities" because you have no control over their performance and therefore should fall into the category of "Equities".

"Tangibles" include gems, metals, collectibles, art, and all your personal belongings including cars, boats and airplanes.

"Fixed income investments" include bonds and long-term bank Certificates of Deposit along with mortgages and other personal loans you might have made to third parties.

"Cash" is money held in savings accounts and money market accounts along with your personal stash of one hundred dollar bills. (See Figure #5)

Since we are always invested, the name of the game becomes that of allocating our investments so that the winning part of our capital outgrows the losing part.

Some Investment Rules:

Here are some rules to follow if you want to beat the investment game and come out a winner:

- Make sure you have no more than 40 percent and no less than 5 percent invested in each of the five categories of assets so that you diversify your risk exposure.
- Adjust your investment positions to reflect the current economic realities.
- Never rely on any one particular investment to make you a profit. Count on the mix of all your investments to keep you ahead of the game.
- Never follow the crowd when making your allocation decisions. When everybody is selling, you should be buying. When everybody is buying, you sell!
- Don't fall in love with your past decisions. Recognize your mistakes early and cut your losses. You will never be 100 percent right about anything.

Keep in mind that no one type of investment is necessarily better than another. The only difference is that you are holding that particular investment. Timing is everything!

Sooner or later, all five investment categories will be hailed as the "best." The name of the game is for you to be holding them before they are recognized as best by the experts.

Most so-called experts are Monday morning quarterbacks. And that leads to the final rule of investment.

- Trust your gut feeling! Chances are if a certain investment position does not "feel" right, it isn't. Don't do it! Use your common sense and intuition to guide you to make the right investment decisions. But make sure you have good solid facts to back that feeling up!

Why Speculate?:

Now let's assume that you have invested all you can into yourself and your family, and you have one years' living expenses sitting in the "cash" category. You have an interest in a closely held business, and you own some income Real Estate and you are ready to tie up some money for the long term in passive investments which are also called "securities."

Stock brokers love to talk about "maximizing investment return." To me, that phrase is an absolute oxy-moron. It falls into the same category as jumbo-shrimp. You are either jumbo or you are a shrimp. Believe me, there is no such thing as "maximizing investment return"!

The only amount of return that you should be getting is "just enough".

One of the first things that you learn when you take investment courses is that risk is commensurate with return. That means that the higher the risk, the higher will be the return. High return without high risk just does not exist. There is no return without risk just as there is no "wealth without risk."

It is true that we are always 100 percent invested, and it is also true that we are subject to risk at all times, but the real question is: "HOW MUCH RISK AND WHAT TYPE OF RISK IS APPROPRIATE FOR OUR SITUATION?"

The answer to that question really determines the amount of return you should be expecting to get on your money.

And my answer is always the same: "JUST ENOUGH!"

For example, if there is no particular need to make 10 percent on your money when money market accounts are paying 4 percent, then 4 percent is a perfectly appropriate return for your capital.

There is no need to expose your capital to additional risk if there is no particular need to receive the extra return. If there is no "need," then the only reason is probably "greed." And that is why most people lose their hard earned dollars in investments, because they allow "greed" to dictate their investment decisions and not "need."

Once again we bump up against the famous word "need."

Remember, markets are pretty efficient, and if one type of investment pays more than another, there is a good reason why this is so. And that reason is risk with a capital R.

Allocating Your Investments:

Now, how do we go about allocating our capital among the various investment categories?

Imagine your capital as a pyramid. The base of the pyramid will have the least "risky" investments. As you go up the pyramid, the investments become riskier, your return becomes greater, and the proportionate amount invested decreases.

Your base of the pyramid will include your bank vehicles, money market funds and short-term government obligations. As you go up the pyramid and you assume more risk, you will have longer-term government obligations, municipal bonds and perhaps corporate high quality bonds. The next rung in the pyramid may include your home, your income Real Estate and your closely held business. Beyond that you are beginning to enter the world of speculation and not really investment, which would include common stocks, Limited Partnership and Reit Shares, Commodities, etc. The tip of the pyramid may include some highly risky venture on which you may decide to take a flyer.

One point to keep in mind is that even though your home and your business may carry more investment risk than municipal bonds, in a sense they really represent less risk because you have much more control over them. They could be considered "use" assets, because you use your business to give you an income for your living expenses, and you live in your home. Therefore their risk is tempered by their utility to you.

By allocating your investments based on a pyramid, that is by having the largest percentage of your assets in the least riskiest categories and the tiniest percentage in the most riskiest, you should achieve a good "average" return. And if you sustain a loss in any one of your investment decisions, chances are that loss will reflect itself in a decrease in return on your total assets rather than a loss to capital. (See Figure #6 and #7)

Measuring Return:

Now that we have talked about risk, let's talk about return.

Most people look at return in absolute terms. That is, they say: "I am getting 10 percent or 15 percent or 20 percent on my money." That to me is a totally meaningless statement.

Return should be tied to two factors: one is time period, the other is inflation. In addition, to really figure out what you are earning, you need to know how much taxes you have to pay on those earnings.

In most instances, if we can generate an after-tax and after-inflation return of 3 percent or so on securities, we can say we are doing very well.

But unfortunately, most "investors" don't do nearly as well. Closely held business and Real Estate can get you much more than that.

Fixed Returns:

Historically, real return on U.S. treasury bonds has been approximately 4 percent over the last couple of hundred years. What I mean by real return is the difference between the current rate of inflation and the yield to maturity that the bond would give you. For example, if you buy an 8 percent coupon bond at par and the current inflation rate is 6 percent, your real return is then 2 percent.

Most people get fooled by returns when they try to measure them in the actual percentage they are getting on their money instead of the difference between inflation and the return.

Ten years ago, when inflation was running in the double digits, you could expect to get 10 percent and 12 percent and more on bonds, money market funds and bank certificates of deposit. However, with inflation running at a higher rate than your return, you were losing money every year. And if you add the taxes you had to pay on your return, it was really costing you a lot of money every year just to keep your money invested. That to me was not good business.

In those days the interest paid was high, but the real rate of return was low, non-existent, and in many cases, negative.

So therefore we can safely say that in those days, real interest rates were low. Yet people are still clamoring for the good old days when you could get 10 percent or 12 percent on your money in the bank.

During the middle to late Eighties, banks and government bonds were paying a low return. During the recessionary early Nineties, money market funds are down to 4 percent and long-term government bonds are at 7.5 percent. Yet the rate of inflation was below 4 percent. That means that real interest rates were at pretty high levels.

When experts say that interest rates are headed higher or lower, I believe them, but not necessarily the way most people may think.

Let me give you some statistics.

Between 1918 and 1939 real interest rates - that is the difference between inflation and bond yield - have averaged 5.3 percent; during the 1950s they were at zero; during the 1960s they were at 2.1 percent; the 1970s at -2 percent and in the late 1980s at 4.7 percent.

You will notice that during periods of high inflation, the real rates were low and during periods of low inflation, real rates were high.

The $64 thousand dollar question is how will interest rates go up or down. Will they go up or down because the nominal rates will fluctuate? Or will they go up or down because inflation will kick up again and even though the nominal rates may go up, the spread between inflation and those rates will decrease?

If the latter occurs, then those who have been pouring their money into-long term bonds or mutual funds that invest in those types of instruments during the times that nominal rates were low, will be taking big losses to their capital because of the interest rate risk.

In addition, if the nominal rates are substantially higher, money will now begin to pour out of stocks and back into bonds, money market funds and bank accounts. So those who have been putting their money into stock mutual funds in order to "get a better return" will probably be taking some heavy losses.

But let's take a look at the direction of interest rates from another perspective.

Our annual national budget deficit for 1992/93 is running at about $400 billion dollars, and it gets worse each year. We have more than $4 trillion in outstanding debt, the interest on which is costing us about 25 percent of our total annual national budget. And this is the case while short term interest rates have been at their lowest levels in twenty-five years.

When our economy recovers from a recession, then the pent up demand for consumer goods, fueled by economic recovery, will push prices higher sometime in the near future. That in turn will place more demand for goods which in turn will push prices even higher.

This means inflation with a capital "I."

This will push long-term interest rates on the open markets much higher.

The Federal Reserve, whose job is to keep tight reign on monetary policies, will also begin to raise short-term interest rates to put a damper on inflation.

But every time we raise interest rates, the government will have to pay out more money for the $4 trillion that it owes.

That means that our deficits will skyrocket regardless of how much we reduce defense spending.

Now here is where I believe our government may pull a fast one on us.

Our government could "inflate" its way out of the budget deficit. This way, the Republicans will blame it on the Democrats and the Democrats will blame it on the Republicans, and Congress and the President will blame it on each other and nobody will be any wiser.

The solution would be very simple. When the economy begins to recover, instead of the Federal Reserve jacking up the short term interest rates to control inflation, it could conveniently fall asleep at the switch, and perhaps even continue to lower the rates.

On top of this, if you throw in a serious across-the-board tax cut, offer investment tax credits, and spend a bundle on public works, you will now have a birthplace for a healthy inflationary "economic recovery".

If you keep short-term rates artificially low, it will be cheaper to borrow than to save, and before you know it, we will be back into double-digit inflation.

But the big question is: "Will it stop there this time as it did back in the early Eighties?"

What if we find ourselves running double-digit inflation rates not annually but monthly, like many Latin American and other countries have experienced in the last twenty years.

Just think! A mere 3 percent per month inflation will cut our three trillion dollar budget deficit by 90 percent in five years.

Of course, it will also cut our savings by the same number, but why not? Nobody will know whose fault it is!

As the famous economist, Milton Friedman put it:

> *Inflation is the one form of taxation that*
> *can be imposed without legislation.*

In view of that philosophy, and some other items we touched on in this chapter, a 4 percent money market return during the recessionary early 90's looks awfully good to me right now simply because your money is loose to swing with the current economic realities rather than being tied up for the long term which, if the above scenario materializes, could make your money disappear.

So, to recap the concept of "return", it is not how much you are getting on your money. It is how much you have left over after inflation and taxes have done their damage that really counts. But that is not all. An equally important question should be, how loose is your money so that you can take advantage of opportunities?

Variable Returns:

> *There is a way to make a lot of money in the market; unfortunately it*
> *is the same way to lose a lot of money in the market.*

PETER PASSELL AND LEONARD ROSE, 1974

Now that we have talked about "fixed income investments" and their returns, let's talk about "equities."

By equities, if we are talking about "securities", we really mean common stocks along with other hybrids like Limited Partnerships etc.

If you were to take any twenty-year period in the history of the stock markets-by which I mean either the Dow Jones Industrial Average or the Standard and Poor's 500 over the last seventy years-you will find that by reinvesting the dividends in that broad market, the most that you could have made would have been about 12 percent and the least would have been about 9 percent. Of this return, about half would have been dividend income and the other half would have been the appreciation of the stock.

That return is somewhat higher than the return you might have enjoyed from bonds, so it is easy to assume that common stocks would give you a better return than bonds.

The problem with making that assumption is that with bonds, your return is fixed, while with stocks its anybody's guess what you might make during any given period in time. The other problem is that for most working people it is impossible to invest in the whole market in the same proportion that all the stocks in the market represent (unless you invest in "Index Funds" but those have their own unique problems).

Therefore, even though the market may be going up, your particular mix of stocks might be going down.

Of course it could go the other way too, that is while the market is going down, your stocks are going up.

The point that I am trying to make is that even though on average you can make a better real return on stocks than you can in bonds, the conditions are such that it is impossible for you to invest in the average. You have to pick individual stocks. And individual stocks do not necessarily track the markets that they compose.

Phrased another way, if you were to place your head in the oven and your feet in the freezer, on average, you would be just right, but in reality you would be dead.

So then the question becomes: "Which stocks should you invest in?"

The answer, of course, is those stocks that will appreciate in value and pay good dividends.

And the next answer is : "Go ahead and find them!"

And when you do, let me know, because I, too, would like to invest in those stocks.

To pick the "right" stocks takes time, knowledge, much statistical information at your disposal, and luck.

Inside every buy there is a sale screaming to get out.

ROBERT HELLER, 1977

Mutual Funds and Money Managers:

Most professional people who work for a living do not have the time to do the research to make their own stock picks. So they find themselves a professional money manager who will do the picking for them.

If you have enough money, you can hire your own private money manager and if you don't, you can always buy into a mutual fund.

The problem is that these people charge a fee to manage your investments. Usually, between the fees and the transaction commissions, you will probably spend about 3 percent of what you have invested.

Subtract this figure now from what you can make from the market on average, and you are left with a return between 6 and 9 percent. That is about what you can get on bonds.

But wait, there is more.

If you track the performance of money mangers, you will find that most of them, perhaps more than 80 percent do not do as well as the markets on average. That means that there is a four out of five chance that you will pick a money manager that over a sustained period of time will give you a lower return than what you can expect from bonds. And in many cases, instead of making money for you, he will lose some of your hard-earned capital.

Of course, if you are lucky, you might pick one that can get you a better return than the market.

But to pick one, you need to do some research and you also need a little luck.

You have more than fifteen thousand such money managers around and there are over three thousand mutual funds to pick from.

Which ones should you invest in?

Once again, if you find one who will make money for you please let me know, because I too would like to place my money with him.

You might say to yourself: "If I just look for a money manager that has a track record of beating the market I will have solved the problem."

The error with that thinking is that past performance is no guarantee of future results. As a matter of fact, most money managers that do very well for a few years usually don't do so well in the next few years. You've got to catch them while they are "hot."

If you are thinking of a mutual fund, how do you know that the person who was able to achieve the spectacular investment result is still working for that mutual fund and hasn't been recruited away to work for somebody else?

There is another problem with mutual funds if you are buying them outside of a tax-sheltered environment.

An important aspect of most mutual funds is that all the transactions that occur within the fund are passed through to the individual mutual fund owners in proportion to their holdings.

That means that as the dividends are received on the stocks held by the fund and as the capital gains are made and realized, those dividends and gains are taxable events to you if you hold that fund.

The problem is that the fund manager may be selling off profitable stock positions and collecting the dividends, yet the stocks that he is holding on to may be losing their value. He may also be reinvesting these gains and dividends into other losers who would continue to slip in value while continuing to sell winners for which you are currently taxed.

That means that you can be paying income taxes while your investment is losing money.

Here is an example: Let's say you invest $10,000 into a mutual fund. If the fund manager sells off the "winners" during the year for, let's say, a $1,000 profit and collects dividends of about $500 during the year, you will have to report $1,500 as ordinary income.

And let's say that the balance of the portfolio that he held on to slipped in value so that your total value of your shares is now only $8,000 which is $2,000 less than what you paid for it.

That means you lost $2,000 while having to pay income taxes on $1,500. This adds to your overall losses and reduces your return on this fund.

So when fund managers calculate their returns, they do not include the gains and dividends you had to pay taxes on while the fund was not making any money. The actual returns to an individual then are, in fact, substantially less than what the fund publishes their return to be.

Now we come to another dilemma related to picking a money manager based on their performance. When money managers publish their performance, they are usually very selective about the things they include and the things they exclude in those calculations. Many times I have seen a mutual fund or a private money manager publish performance results that did not match the returns that the individual participant got on his portfolio. The reasons for this are many, one being that a private money manager may specifically exclude certain accounts from his performance results and pick only the best performing accounts for his report.

A mutual fund or a private money manager may pick only certain periods of time that are most favorable to the performance to publish their results. They may exclude transaction commissions and management fees from the results. The best performance could have been obtained during a few short years while the fund had very little money in it. Later, when the fund had a substantial amount to invest, the performance might have been just ordinary, but the high returns during the early years may be reflecting the funds official performance over the long term.

My Broker Picks the Winning Stocks for Me:

A broker is a man who runs your fortune into a shoestring.

ALEXANDER WOOLLCOTT, 1935

After reading all this about mutual funds and private money managers, you might now say to yourself: "I don't need to find me a money manager or buy a mutual fund, I'll just make things simple and rely on my broker's recommendations on the stocks I should buy."

That is probably the worst thing you can do.

To begin with, your broker spends most of his or her time selling securities and not doing research on stocks as does the money manager.

Of course, large brokerage houses have their own research departments and they do put out stock recommendations. The problem is that those same brokerage houses also have a huge conflict of interest in some of those recommendations. Most brokerage houses are what you call "market makers" in certain stocks. Translated that means that they are committed to keeping the price of the stock high. They buy and sell for their own account and make profits on the gains of their stock picks. What this could mean is that when your stockbroker calls you and tells you to buy a certain stock, the brokerage house has already made its profit on this stock and is unloading the stock to you, the customer, before the price goes down. Or it could mean that there is significant selling pressure on a stock that the brokerage house is making a market in, and since the house doesn't have very much confidence in the company, instead of buying up the shares for the house account as it is supposed to do, it is spreading some of its risk with the public.

Or it could mean that the brokerage house has committed itself to push a certain company stock because it was named as an underwriter for that issue.

In addition, brokerage houses like to maintain good relationships with the companies whose stocks they trade because they want to keep them as future customers for underwriting their stock and bond issues. For that reason, they only like to publish positive information in their research reports on companies.

When you read a brokerage house research report, you will notice a lot of reasons why you should buy the stock of the company they are recommending. However, I have yet to see similar information about a company which might convince you to sell the stock of that company. Since we all know that stocks go up and down, what good is it to know when to buy the stock of a company if you don't get information about when to sell the stock of that same company?

So much for brokerage house research reports.

Why take the risk?

Now after hearing all this you might say to yourself: "Why go into all this trouble and take so much risk just to perhaps make a little bit more than what I could get in bonds or in the bank?"

After spending a quite a few years in the investment advisory business, I, too, began asking myself the same question.

One way to confirm this, is to ask the money manger or your stock broker to show you a copy of the brokerage house report that shows where they have their money invested. You'd be surprised to find how many of these "stock gurus" keep their money somewhere else.

Now, of course, to be fair, I have only been talking so far about the risks related to investment in stocks and have not touched on the rewards.

To be sure, there are many rewards. Even if over 80 percent of the money managers can't get you a better return than 9 percent to 12 percent on your money over the long haul, the other 10 percent of the money managers can get you a nice hefty premium over that figure. The idea is to find the one who will make money for you. And believe me, that is not easy unless you have a crystal ball.

The whole point of this discussion about stocks is to emphasize that in order to get a better return, you have got to assume a much greater risk.

You need to ask yourself whether this risk to your capital is really worth the extra return. If it isn't why do it? Life is too short to spend sleepless nights worrying about what your money is doing. At least for me it is. You may be different.

But one thing is for sure. Greed is definitely one of the forces that works against us and takes our capital away when we are not looking. Investing in common stocks, you will have plenty of opportunity to come face-to-face with Mr. Greed. And in most instances, Mr. Greed wins and you lose.

Is it not odd that the only generous person I ever knew, who had money to be generous with, should be a stockbroker.

PERCY BYSSHE SHELLEY, 1822

Limited Partnerships:

There is one area that falls into the category of "securities" that we need to discuss. Those represent Limited Partnerships.

There are many types of LP's that have been set up, including oil and gas, real estate, equipment leasing, farming and ranching, cable TV etc. Most of them have lost money.

Before I continue, however, I would like to mention that when I talked about the category of investment that represents Real Estate, I was not referring to public offerings of real estate Limited Partnerships. I was specifically referring to real estate, either commercial or residential, personally owned and managed.

To me a real estate Limited Partnership is not an investment in Real Estate but a speculation on the integrity and the competence of the project sponsor or General Partner.

For my money, investment in Real Estate is totally different than an investment in a real estate LP. Those two are like night and day.

For those who are not familiar with these investments, LP's are generally nonliquid because you can't cash out until a specific time has elapsed or until the General Partner decides it is time to cash out. In some cases, like oil and gas income programs, you never cash out, all you get is the income stream until the oil and gas runs out.

The idea here is that the GP runs the business and the partnership and has all the liability, while you, the Limited Partner, invest your money and hope that the GP makes money for you.

The best way to figure out whether these are good investments or not is to take a look and see how many of them made money, how much money and how many of them didn't do so well.

There are a dozen or so firms nationwide that create a secondary market for these partnerships. Therefore, the prices that these partnerships are selling for on the open market should be a pretty good indication of their current values.

From a recent listing out of some 250 partnerships that changed hands in a month, only 10 of them sold for more than what the investor had originally paid for them. Out of those ten, seven were Cable TV companies. Since there were 15 cable companies listed, that means that out of the basket of 235 different types of Partnerships, only 3 were worth more than what the investor had paid for them.

That has been pretty much par for the course in Limited Partnerships.

I have heard many excuses given for this poor performance, including blaming the Tax Reform Act of 1986 that killed most of the deductions related to real estate deals. But the real reason I believe that these Limited Partnerships have not been doing so well is because of the structure itself.

In many partnerships, the General Partners took out their profits up front out of the investment collected from the LP's and then just walked away from the project because they no longer had an incentive to make it profitable. Some GP's sold their own land to the Partnership at a profit and then walked away. Others had many conflicts of interest with the partnership and made their money through side fees charged to the partnership for various services rather that making the partnership profitable.

Of course, each investor had the opportunity to review this when they were given the offering memorandum, because all these conflicts of interest were usually disclosed. But then, who reads these big thick boring looking papers anyway?

Real Estate:

Now let's talk about Real Estate. To me investment in Real Estate means physically purchasing a commercial or a residential property, collecting the rent on it, paying off the mortgage and then using the net income to improve or maintain my standard of living, ad infinitum. This process is not a passive investment or a "security," but is a combination of both "money at work" and "man at work." You are actually going into the business of owning Real Estate. And that is the only way I feel one should own Real Estate.

If you invest in Real Estate Limited Partnerships or Real Estate Investment Trusts, you are really giving up most of the opportunities for profit to the sponsors of the projects, yet you are assuming all the risks. To me, this risk reward ratio just does not make sense.

From my perspective, if you really want to make money in Real Estate, you better be ready to worry about stuffed toilets. And if you are willing to accept that responsibility, then the returns you will see will generally dwarf anything that you can possibly make through most passive investments or "securities."

An important point to keep in mind is that much of the profits you make in Real Estate are made when you purchase the property. Don't buy the property because you like it. Buy it because the seller has to sell for some personal reason and is willing to give it to you for a good price. Don't be afraid to make a low ball offer and if the seller refuses to sell, walk away from the deal.

Take short mortgages. Don't try to "finance out" the property. This way you will be paying down principal and converting income to capital. Don't worry about negative cash flows if you can afford the difference and if your principal paydown is greater than your out of pocket outlay. You are creating forced savings.

An important point to keep in mind when purchasing investment Real Estate is to make sure the investment makes "Financial Sense."

For example, as a rule of thumb, you should never pay more than ten times annual rent for a piece of property. That means if the potential rental income is $2,500 per month, your price for this property should not exceed $300,000. Ideally, if the property is in good condition the price should be 8 to 9 times rent. If the property is old and needs work, it should sell for 3 to 6 times rent (depending on its condition and occupancy).

Many people have purchased residential property in areas where values were appreciating quickly with the hope of making a profit on the resale even though the rent multiple didn't make sense. Forget that idea.

That's not investment, that's speculation!

By the time you get through paying closing fees, taxes and Real Estate commissions and the cost of carrying the property, you will have eaten up all your profit and taken a hefty loss-even if you sell that property for 50 percent more than you paid for it a couple years later.

Just remember this: THE ONLY WAY TO VALUE INVESTMENT REAL ESTATE IS BY ITS POTENTIAL RENT MULTIPLE AND 10 IS MY LIMIT.

On the other hand, if you buy a home that you like and enjoy, even though its potential rent multiple maybe much more than 10, don't worry about it. The property then becomes your "use asset" and its value is measured not in how much profit you get from it but by how much pleasure it gives you to live there.

If you can afford it, buy it and enjoy it!

Inflation Adjusted Income is the Answer:

Most important of all, Real Estate should be bought, not sold because Real Estate represents a source of inflation adjusted income.

The income stream from one million dollars worth of Real Estate will be much greater than the same million dollars invested in financial assets.

For example, if you have a property that is worth one million dollars and, assuming it has no mortgage, after paying the miscellaneous maintenance expenses it is giving you $80,000 per year annually. This $80,000 will probably increase periodically and chances are the increases will parallel inflation.

If you sold this building and invested the million dollars in financial assets, and if the inflation rate is 5 percent and let's say you average 8 percent on your money invested in financial assets, then your net return will be only $30,000 per year. But let's say that you decided to take out $80,000 per year and you increased that income to yourself at the same rate as the inflation rate. In 17 years your principal will be totally depleted. Yet if you had kept the building and if it appreciated at the rate of inflation, you would still have the building which by now would be giving you an income of $175,000 annually and its value would be $2.3 million dollars.

Of course, remember, the building is a combination of "man at work" and "money at work" whereas, dollars invested in financial assets are strictly "money at work."

If it looks like you have too much equity in your properties and they represent more than 40 percent of your net worth, then refinance the property and place the money elsewhere. You may not make as much on it as your cost of the mortgage, but your reason for doing it is then diversification of your capital. This is just good insurance but it may cost you. The upside is that as long as the mortgage you take out is a short one, you are back to converting income to capital. And conversion of income to capital is a key element in your quest for financial independence.

Before I got smart, I used to chase after every investment scheme that any broker would present me. I invested in Mutual Funds, in Limited Partnerships, in Real Estate Investment Trusts, in Options, in Futures, and I even bought an occasional lottery ticket.

Somehow, no matter what I did, there was some kind of unforseen problem and I wound up losing all or some of my principal.

Today, my asset allocation is very simple. 35 percent in individually owned net real estate equity, 5 percent tangibles, 15 percent in controlling closely held business interests that give me an income with a minimal amount of "man at work" requirement, and 45 percent in U.S. Treasury Bonds, Municipal Bonds and cash.

What about the Limited Partnership or the Stockmarket? Perhaps I might come in with up to 10 percent or 20 percent of my net worth at the right moment. But right now, why bother?

And here is why not.

History and The "Dow":

The Dow Jones Industrials hit 1,000 for the first time in 1966. It took the Dow 16 years, until 1982, before it broke out and went higher. It got close to 3,000 back in 1987. It's been bouncing around that number for almost five years now. It'll be a few more years, I believe, before it will significantly break out of the 3,000 range and the market may even go down some before it makes its move foreward.

The reason is that during the last ten years we have had the biggest bull market in modern history, representing an average annual increase of over 14 percent. If historically all we can expect from the market is 9 percent to 12 percent, (including dividend reinvestment) then we have a few more years to go before those numbers average themselves out.

Okay, maybe I'll miss out on some profits. But, once again I remind myself of our founding father Benjamin Franklin, who once said:

"I am more interested in the return of my money
than on the return on it!"

So I sleep nights and enjoy my skiing. Happy investing!

It wasn't raining when Noah built the ark.

HOWARD RUFF, 1980

MONEY AT WORK
- only two places for -
CAPITAL

	OWN	LOAN
RISKS	Market	Interest
	Business	Business
	Obsolescence	Inflation
REWARDS	Maintain Value	Fixed Principal
	Return Commensurate with Productivity	Fixed Return

FIGURE #4

FIVE INVESTMENT CATEGORIES

LOAN

1. Fixed Instruments
   Bonds
   Bank Certificates
   Mortgages

2. Cash
   Money Market Funds
   Bank Accounts

OWN

1. Equities
   Common Stocks
   Closely Held Business
   Limited Partnership & Reit Shares

2. Real Estate
   Land/Commercial/Residential
   Rental Income

3. Tangibles
   Metals
   Collectibles
   Gems

FIGURE #5

RISK TO CAPITAL CLASSIFICATION

Speculative
(Almost Gamble)

Options
Futures
Venture
Capital

High Risk

Common Stocks
Limited Partnerships

Medium Risk

Closely Held Business
Real Estate

Low Risk

Corporate Bonds
Insurance/Annuities
Municipal Bonds

Minimal
Risk

Treasury Backed Sec.
Insured Bank Inst.

FIGURE #6

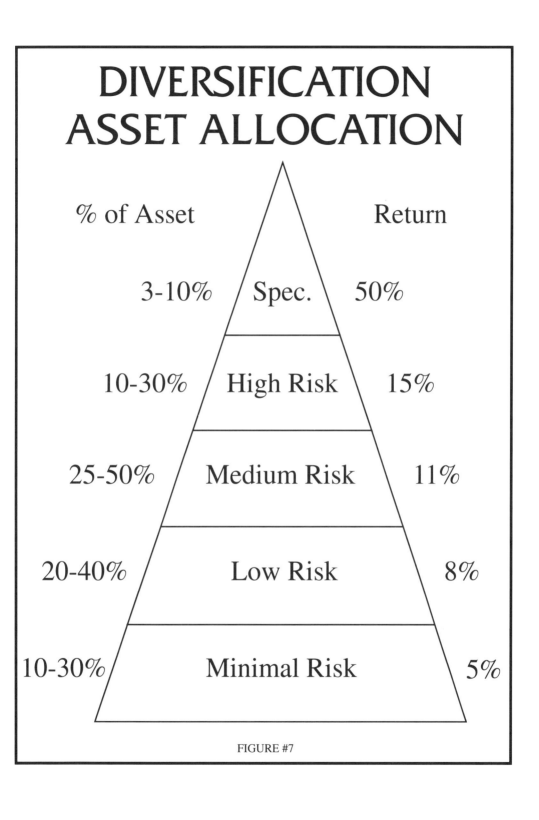

DIVERSIFICATION
ASSET ALLOCATION

% of Asset   Return

3-10%   Spec.   50%

10-30%   High Risk   15%

25-50%   Medium Risk   11%

20-40%   Low Risk   8%

10-30%   Minimal Risk   5%

FIGURE #7

It's a great country, but you can't live in it for nothing.

WILL ROGERS, 1929

Nothing is to be had for nothing.

EPICTETUS, c. A.D. 138

The buyer needs a hundred eyes, the seller not one.

GEORGE HERBERT, 1640

This guy Marx, why, he was one of these efficiency experts. He could explain to you how you could save a million dollars, yet he couldn't save enough himself to eat on.

WILL ROGERS, 1929

CHAPTER 12

Commissions can cost us more than we think

UNFORTUNATELY, WE CANNOT GO THROUGH LIFE without purchasing financial products. By financial products I mean any kind of financial service or investment that some third party places at the disposal of the general public.

The problem is that every time we buy any financial product, the person who is guiding us through the process has something to gain by selling us his particular type of product.

In other words, the advice we may be getting from the person who is supposedly "advising" us on what we should get is, generally speaking, slanted in favor of making someone a commission rather than making us, the customers, a profit or saving money.

Specifically, every time we want to buy insurance, take out a consumer loan, refinance our house or take out a new mortgage, purchase stocks, bonds, mutual funds, buy some real estate, place our money in a bank Certificate of Deposit, or just finance our car, the person who is telling us what we should be buying is profiting from our decision.

Most of us don't realize the amount of money we spend on "commissions" every year.

To give you an example, let's say that in one year you decide to purchase a new, $30,000 Volvo through a lease program, sell your old house for $150,000 and buy a new $200,000 house with a $150,000 mortgage, buy homeowners insurance plus purchase life and disability insurance policies for which you are paying $500 per month and, you decide to follow the advice of your broker and place $50,000 into mutual funds.

Have you thought about how much you will be paying in commissions on all of these transactions?

Of course, commission rates vary, and in many instances, you can negotiate the amount of commissions you pay, but a good ball park estimate is that during that year, you probably paid out between $35,000 and $40,000 of commissions to somebody.

That means probably one-half or one-third of your net salary that year (if you are buying a $200,000 house that's where you would be) went to pay someone a commission. And that is not counting the cost of the product itself or the cost of interest to finance those products that you did not pay for with cash.

And you wonder where your money goes?

Of course, you can reduce, and, in many instances, eliminate many of these commissions by either dealing directly with the sellers or negotiating a lower commission with the salesperson or institution.

But that is not the real problem.

The real problem is that, in many instances, we tend to take the "advice" of the person who is selling us the item and allow them to dictate to us what we should be buying.

In many instances, after paying all those commissions, we wind up making purchases that have a negative effect on our capital because we may buy not that which is right for us, but that item where the salesperson makes the most amount of money.

Not that there is anything wrong with the system. If it weren't for commissions, the products may not exist because there might not be anyone there to sell them. But in order for us to defend ourselves, we need to know whose advice we are taking and what is motivating that person to give the advice to us.

For example, the life insurance agent will always try to sell you some form of "whole life" or "universal life" type policy. He or she will come up with reams of proposals that will prove to you beyond a shadow of a doubt that this is the ONLY way to buy your insurance.

I used to brainwash my agents to do this because this is how I, as a General Agent, made the most money. I even used to penalize agents that didn't take this approach to selling insurance.

As a matter of fact, I was so good at it that, as a result, instead of having to slave away at some job, I can be writing this book.

The only reason I am saying this is to illustrate the point of how you, as the consumer, can wind up throwing away thousands of your hard earned dollars on insurance products just because the agent has a greater incentive to sell them rather than those products that you really need and which are a lot cheaper and better for you.

Let's get down to dollars and cents. If you buy a "whole life" or "universal life" policy, where you pay premiums of $500 monthly, the total commission the agent can earn on this policy over a ten- year period will range between $6,000 and $9,000 depending on the company that he or she represents.

If you buy the equivalent amount of Term insurance, the commission will probably not exceed $1,000 and will more than likely be less than $500.

After spending twenty very successful years in the business, I can emphatically state to you that there are very few reasons why you should be buying "whole life" insurance, when you can be buying plain simple (and cheap) term insurance.

Just about everything that "whole life" can do, "term" can do better and cheaper.

And if you buy your insurance in certain states like California and Florida, which allow rebating, you can negotiate the commissions that the agent will earn on your purchase.

Another area that lends itself to a lot of abuse because of commissions is securities.

Stock brokers don't make their money by making money for their customers. They make money by making transactions. To a stock broker there is no incentive for a certain stock he sells to you to go up or down. But he does have an incentive to have you buy and sell the stock.

For that reason, the worst thing you can do is give a stock broker discretionary rights over your account.

We talked about this in a previous chapter, but a stockbroker is not your "advisor." His job is not to do research on the stock market and determine which might be the best companies to invest in. That is the job of the "money manager." The stockbroker's job is to make a transaction, and anything that he may say to you in order to accomplish that end result is okay. He is a salesperson of securities not someone who advises you where you should invest your money. That you will have to determine yourself.

And that brings us to the next breed of financial products salesperson.

Namely, the "Financial Planner."

This is probably the most dangerous type of securities and insurance person you can come up against.

Like most people, you are probably very busy with your work and, don't really have time to do all the research necessary to figure out what the best investment or insurance alternatives might be. So you need an "advisor" to show you these alternatives.

This places you in a very vulnerable position, because you are entrusting your hard-earned dollars to someone who may be profiting very handsomely by telling you which investments you may hold and what insurance policies you should buy. For that reason, you want to be sure that the person from whom you are getting this advice is both competent and, above all, objective.

"Financial Planners" have been around for about twenty years now, but I didn't really get wind of this wrinkle until 1980 or 1981.

It was brought to my attention by the insurance company I represented then in Puerto Rico.

The theory went something like this: Since there are a lot of busy people out there that need advice and don't have the time to do their own research, the insurance company would set up a separate department in the Home Office which it called the Financial Planning Department. This department would give technical back up to each individual Agency (like the one I had in Puerto Rico) in developing Financial Planning within their operation.

For those of you who may not be fully familiar with what "Financial Planning" really is, here is a quick explanation: It is a service that involves coordinating all the different aspects of a clients personal finances and having them form a part of a master plan. Those aspects included Managing Personal Cash Flow, Analyzing Insurance Needs, Managing Investments, Tax Planning and Estate Distribution Planning. Since the service involves a considerable amount of work by the person who is performing this "planning" service, there is usually a fee charged to the customer.

When my company first introduced the program we were to implement in our Agencies, the person presenting it to us said: "As an insurance company, we were traditionally able to take care of our customers 'from the womb to the tomb.' Now, with Financial Planning, we will take care of them 'from the erection to the resurrection.'"

My job was then to appoint a sales manager within my agency who would act as the Financial Planning liaison between my brokers and insurance agents and their customers.

Under this system, all of my 160 or so sales representatives became instant "Financial Planners."

We could now easily go into a client, tell him we are not really selling insurance and securities, but instead we are acting as his "advisors," and by gaining the customer's confidence, we were able to load them up with high commission insurance and securities products.

The gimmick worked like a charm, and not just in our operation but all over the country. And we weren't the only company on the block cashing in on this new "advice" bonanza.

Just about every insurance company and brokerage house suddenly sprouted "Financial Planning" departments that were charging fees for their "financial planning services," plus hauling in the commissions for all the insurance and securities that their "advisors" were now able to push without the usual salespitch.

I've got to hand it to them. They came up with a real booster to their bottom line on this one.

But I wasn't complaining in those days. I was in there with the rest of the bunch, hauling in the bucks and lining my pockets.

There was nothing illegal about what was being done, but it was definitely pushing the limits of ethics and fair play.

Here was a customer, believing that he was getting objective advice while all the while he was being given a sales pitch cleverly masked as a unique service.

Within a short time I realized that "Financial Planning" or "Personal Financial Counseling" could be a valuable service in and by itself as long as objectivity was maintained by not having the person who was giving the advice receive commissions on his or her own recommendations. That was the only way it could be truly done as a service, and not just a gimmick to sell insurance and securities.

Recently, the Securities and Exchange Commission has been taking a close look at this "self dealing" position and has come out with special regulations to reduce the many abuses that have been going on by "Financial Planners" over the years. I don't believe they went far enough.

In my opinion, the worst example of this abusive practice is exemplified by some of the holders of the designation C.F.P., or Certified Financial Planner.

This designation is offered through a self-study program by an organization out of Denver, Co. called "The College for Financial Planning."

Anyone can obtain this designation as long as they pass the six exams given by the college and meet other criteria. The study materials and the course itself are excellent because it gives those who go through the program much technical information about Securities, Insurance, Taxes, Wills and Trusts, along with basics in Retirement Planning, Personal Financial Accounting and business Evaluation.

I went through the course and received my designation and became a "C.F.P." in 1985. But the truth is that now I am often ashamed to admit that I am a "C.F.P."

Much prestige hype and publicity has been printed exalting the holders of this designation, and many unscrupulous fast-buck operators have taken advantage of this to position themselves as "advisors" to their clients. In fact, often their only interest is loading their customers up with high commission, questionable and sometimes fraudulent securities, and other investments.

I am not saying that all C.F.P.'s fall into this category, nor am I saying that everyone who is a "Financial Planner/C.F.P." and also sells financial products is dishonest or unethical. There are many C.F.P.'s who are also product sales people that are dedicated to their profession and honestly want to do the right thing for their clients. What I am saying is that it is very difficult for Mr. Joe Public to determine who is the crook, once the C.F.P. label has been paraded before him.

At first I tried to isolate this "Financial Planning" service within my organization by funneling the program through a separate corporation.

But the problem always arose when the time came to make an analysis and make recommendations to a client. If those recommendations did not include the purchase of insurance or securities, my brokers would get mad and threaten to do their business elsewhere. So I was between a rock and a hard place. If I tried to offer an objective analysis to the clients through this service, and not include high- priced insurance and securities products as part of the recommendations, my brokers would walk out on me and I would be out of business.

It would always come down to asking myself the same question: "What business am I in?" The only answer that made sense at the time was: "I am in the insurance and securities business, and Financial Planning is just a fringe benefit that I am offering to my clients so that I can sell more products."

Therefore, all my "recommendations" had to include the purchase of securities and insurance as a solution regardless of what the client's real problem happen to be.

Now, having left the insurance and securities business, and having worked for about eight years as a fee-only Financial Planner (not accepting any commissions or referral fees directly or indirectly for the recommendations I make to a client), I realized that insurance and securities represent less than five percent of the work I do for a client. Yet when I was running my insurance agency and broker/dealer business, ninety-five percent of the recommendations in my "Financial Planning Department" centered around the purchase of insurance and securities.

Now, that is not to say that there aren't people out there who honestly try to do the right job of Financial Planning and still sell their customers financial products. What I am saying is that if you are in a position to deal yourself a nice commission in the process of offering a service, you might very well be swayed in making that commission very lucrative to yourself in detriment to your client if your rent happens to be due this month.

Also, if your bread and butter is commissions and less than five percent of "Financial Planning" involves the purchase of securities and insurance, why should you do the other 95 percent of the work?

That is precisely why, in January of 1985, I decided to give up all my licenses to sell any financial products and began my fee-only Financial Counseling firm.

Of course, by that time I had already built a nice nest egg of capital -which I made by doing all these things I am saying in this chapter shouldn't be done- so making a lot of money was no longer a priority.

Would I have been so brave and virtuous had I not had the money in the bank? I'll never know the real answer to that one. However, I do know that we fallable human beings are driven by necessity and not altruism, and in those days I still had two kids in school.

And that is precisely why, if you are going to listen to any advice, be sure that whoever is giving it to you has nothing else to gain except the fee he or she may be charging you for that advice.

One thing you should keep in mind. Your stockbroker, your Real Estate agent, your insurance agent, your banker, even though they make money by you following their "advice," do have some good information to share with you. You should listen to what they have to say because you can learn a great deal from their input. However, remember, they are making money off you if you do what they suggest. Sometimes, what they suggest may not be in your best interest, and the reason they are saying it is because they stand to profit by you acting on what they say. Remember: Caveat Emptor! Buyer Beware!

But I don't want to be unfair. There are many people who live from commissions who are very ethical and honest and really do try to do the best for their customers. However, it is up to you to find those people if you want the "best" advice and that is very tough to do. Sometimes the ones who appear on the surface as the most honest, are really clever salespeople who know how to masquerade as "wolves in sheeps clothing."

You will also find that many insurance agents and stockbrokers like to impress their customers by appearing successful.

Many of them drive fancy cars, live in the best neighborhoods and wear expensive clothes and jewelry.

Don't be impressed with the outward appearances. It's all part of the hype!

Just because someone is earning a lot of money in the financial services field doesn't necessarily mean that they are earning those dollars by being straight and honest with their customers.

On the contrary, it could be the opposite. It could be that they are earning all those dollars because they are doing something that may not be in their customer's best interest. But because they are such strong sales personalities, they are able to sell "two milking machines to a farmer who only has one cow and then take the cow as the down payment."

Check out their references before you do business with them. And don't talk to their banker or their accountant. Talk to their customers, and not those who are their satisfied customers but those who are not so satisfied with what they have done for them.

But most important of all, ask to see their personal financial statements. Especially if you are working with a "Financial Planner."

Make sure that they are doing for themselves what they are recommending to you.

How can you possibly take the advice of someone who is supposedly going to help you get rich if they themselves are not "rich?"

If they won't take their own advice, why should you take theirs.

Since your stockbroker, your insurance agent and your "Financial Planner" will all, sooner or later, know intimately what your personal finances are, shouldn't you know what their personal finances are if you are going to listen to them and follow their advice?

You have every right to know! And if they won't tell you, don't do business with them!

I started this chapter by talking about how commissions can be a catalyst for you to squander your hard earned capital. Well, no matter how hard you try, you will never be able to get away from someone who might have a big incentive -making a commission- to sell you something that you may not need or want.

The name of the game is not to try to get away from commissions, because you can't. Instead, the idea is to recognize why someone is suggesting you do something and act accordingly.

As the famous showman P.T. Barnum once said:

"There is a sucker born every minute."

Just make sure you are not one of them!

The cost of living has gone up another dollar a quart.

W.C. FIELDS, 1937

We know now that inflation results from all that deficit spending.

RONALD REAGAN, 1981

Inflation might also be called legal counterfeiting.

IRVING FISHER, 1928

Though the wages of the workman are commonly paid to him in money, his real revenue, like that of all other men, consists, not in money, but in the money's worth, not in the metal pieces, but in what can be got for them.

ADAM SMITH, 1776

The power of taxation by currency depreciation is one which has been inherent in the State since Rome discovered it.

JOHN MAYNARD KEYNES, 1933

CHAPTER 13

Reasonable inflation?
No such thing!

OVER THE LAST TEN YEARS OR SO, I am willing to bet, your income has probably doubled, tripled and perhaps even quadrupled or more, however, I am also willing to bet that your debts are higher than they have ever been, and that you have less in savings as a percentage of your earned income than what you did five or ten years ago. But not only that. If you are like most Americans, you are having a tougher time paying your bills today, even with this increased income, than what you did just a few short years ago.

Do you remember when you were earning $2,000 per month, you would say to yourself: "If I could only earn $3,000 per month I could pay back all my debts and my problems will be solved." And when your income went to $50,000 per year, you would say that if only your salary could be increased to $75,000 you would be on easy street.

The problem is that, unless you do something to prevent it, your spending patterns will expand with your income regardless of whether you are earning one hundred thousand dollars per year or one million.

But don't feel guilty. It is not entirely your fault. There are forces out there that prevent you from creating and keeping your capital. Some of them are internal and some of them are external.

One external force is inflation. There is nothing you can do to reduce it. However you can do things to minimize it. When you add the element of taxes to this equation, the progression of gross earned income needed to keep up with expanding costs is almost geometric.

This phenomenon is called "Taxflation."

But first, let's talk about just plain ordinary inflation.

Let's say you have just graduated from college and you land a job with a medium-sized company that pays you $20,000 per year. In eight years you become a middle manager and your salary is $42,871, a 10 percent annual increase in pay. Let's say this 10 percent increase continues and by the time you are 38, you become a "general manager" earning $91,897 per year; a Vice President at 45 earning $179,081 per year; a senior VP at 52 earning $348,978 per year; and you retire as President of the company at age 62 earning $905,159 per year. (See Figure #8)

Even though all this seems like a meteoric rise to riches, your income has really only increased by 10 percent per year since you started.

At first you might say that this is pretty good progression. But now let's see what 6 percent inflation would do to your income.

When you finally retire 40 years later, your $905,185 income as president would have been only $88,003 in real dollars at 6 percent inflation. Or phrased another way, if you wanted to maintain a real 10 percent increase in salary on top of inflation over this forty year period, your income would have to have been $7,574,418 in the year that you retired. (See Figure #9)

And that is only taking inflation into consideration, not the taxes that you would have to pay on the gross increase.

Now let's bring this problem a little closer to home and see what your earnings would have to be if inflation continues at an average rate of about 6 percent (which it has been for the last 15 years) and you are in the 33 percent tax bracket with an income of $60,000 this year.

Well, in five years your income would have to be $102,300. In ten years it would have to be $159,600. In fifteen years, it would have to be $248,940 and in twenty years it would have to be $388,306. (See Figure #10)

You have to keep in mind that these salary increases would only keep you even with inflation. These income increases will not pay for a new baby, a bigger house, a bigger car, a new boat, or alimony payments. This is what you have to earn just to stay even.

If you want any extras over and above what you have now, your income increases would have to be proportionately higher.

Would your boss be so understanding to make sure your income needs kept up with this "taxflation"?

I doubt it, and statistics prove this out.

Based on a survey of 1990 incomes over 1989 incomes, it appears that the two-earner median income increased to $51,421 in 1990 from the 1989 level of $49,090.

However, because of a $582 tax increase and a 5 percent inflation that year, this family earned $614 less in 1990 than in 1989.

Over a longer period of time the picture is worse. Over the last 15 years, our incomes have declined in real terms by approximately 20 percent.

Some experts believe that inflation has been beaten and is no longer a problem.

I think as long as inflation exists, even in the five or six percent range it may not be a problem to the experts, but to the average American family it is a real killer.

Here is another example. Let's say that you are that young man who was very successful and worked his way up from a trainee to the president of the company with your income increasing at a 10 percent rate as you went through the various positions of the company. And let's also say that you were quite frugal and were able to save ten percent of your gross income each year.

In 40 years, or your age 62, you would have accumulated $2,632,269 assuming that your return on investment was 8 percent.

Well, at an inflation rate of 6 percent, this two and a half million dollars would only be worth $255,913 in today's, or constant, dollars.

What that means is that even if you were able to save that 10 percent of gross income over a 40-year period, it probably wouldn't even take care of your retirement. For example, if you wanted to have an income from age 62 to your life expectancy of age 77, with an inflation rate of 6 percent, you could only draw the equivalent of about $1800 per month assuming your return on investment was 8 percent net after taxes.

Is that any way to retire?

But we don't have to look at just a bunch of hypothetical situations. Let's look at something closer to the situation you may be in right now. Say you are now participating in a 401k plan that will give you $500,000 when you retire in twenty-five years. At 6 percent inflation, this half a million dollars will be worth only about $116,499. After you subtract one-third for the taxes you will have to pay, your actual use of this money will be down to less than $80,000.

If you want this $80,000 to give you a retirement income of $2,000 per month in today's dollars, then the money will last for only about three and a half years at a 6 percent inflation rate and an 8 percent net return on your capital.

What kind of retirement is that?

Yes, "taxflation" is an external force that keeps you broke no matter how hard you try to save your money for the future. That is if all you do is stick to traditional forms of creating capital such as plain savings as a fixed percentage of your income. You need to have other things going for you than just a company retirement plan and an I.R.A. if you want to reach a certain level of financial independence.

The first and the most obvious one is to be lucky enough (as was our Mr. Executive in a previous chapter) to have progressed quickly within your corporation so that your income increased faster than the rate of "taxflation." Now if instead of living and spending like Mr. Executive you had the presence of mind to hold back on increasing your standard of living commensurate with your salary increases and save the excess, then your increased capital at work will be buying you all the extra "goodies." And then you will have enough capital to become independent of earned income.

This doesn't mean that you have to spend the rest of your life in a rented two bedroom walk up. But what it does mean is that whenever your income takes a jump rather than a modest percentage increase, you need to give it a couple of years of lag time before you allow your spending habits to catch up to your income.

This way you stay out of debt, and even though eventually you wind up with all the "toys" that go with the income, the excess saved over a couple of years begins to significantly increase your capital base. This extra little edge, when compounded over the years, will make a big difference.

In a previous chapter I talked about how a source of inflation adjusted income is worth more than its equivalent dollar amount invested in financial assets such as stocks, bonds and bank certificates.

This source of inflation adjusted income can only come from two sources. Those are: owning a closely held business that you control and from real estate that you own and manage personally.

Any business ownership where you do not have controlling interest, will not accomplish the job for you and any real estate that you own through either a limited partnership or a REIT, is nothing more than another form of financial asset, where the bulk of the profits are eaten up by the real estate project sponsors and you are left with only the crumbs.

Your own business and individually owned Real Estate allow you to accumulate capital at an accelerated rate because they are a combination of "man at work" and "capital at work," and also because they combine, tax benefits with paydown of principal and capital appreciation.

This triple whammy combination, allows for your capital to grow at a geometric procession rate rather than simple numerical compounding.

Here is an example. Let's say you purchase a closely held business. Your price will probably be about three or four times annual net before tax profits (unless the business has substantial capital assets such as machinery or Real Estate). You will probably put one third down and the other two thirds will be financed by probably the seller and the bank.

If you do something to increase the profits, your income above the debt paydown could be 50 percent or more of your down payment.

Within three or four years you would have paid off the other two thirds of the purchase price, and after that your net before tax income from the business could be 150 percent or more of your down payment.

If you can save this income because you have another source of earned income, your savings rate could then be 150 percent of your down payment (less tax) plus the rate of appreciation in value of your business.

Of course, you have to supervise the manager of the business, you have to take the risks related to business ownership and you have to be responsible for the lines of credit you owe to the banks, but that is all part of "man at work." Most of your time is spent in thinking out the solutions to problems and not necessarily physically slaving away in the business.

This analogy could apply to most small businesses ranging from a "mom and pop" retail store to an assembly plant with 100 or more employees.

In Real Estate, the process is very similar. You purchase real estate, take a short mortgage, pay down principal, perhaps use some of your other earned income to help with the mortgage paydown (this is forced savings), you collect the rents and when the mortgage is paid off, you refinance and start the process all over again on the same property. You are converting income to capital through mortgage paydown and if your real estate appreciates in value, your savings are multiplied by that factor.

If you buy a piece of property for $300,000 and put $75,000 down and take a fifteen-year mortgage of $225,000 on it, chances are you can rent it for $2,500 per month. This should take care of most of the expenses. If that rent increases by 3 percent each year over the next ten years, you should be collecting $3,300 monthly. If you put the difference between what you collect and your expenses back into the mortgage, chances are you will have the property paid off within that ten-year period.

If the property appreciates at, let's say, 3 percent each year, then at the end of ten years, you will have a piece of real estate property fully paid off that will be worth about $400,000.

So you see that by combining "man at work" with your $75,000 of "capital at work" you have increased the value of your $75,000 to $400,000 within about a ten year period. Plus, you now have an inflation adjusted source of income of $3,300 that you can use to either reinvest or buy you that Jaguar you always wanted.

You will notice, nowhere did I attempt to measure the amount of profit you might have made on that piece of real estate. The reason is that the actual return on investment is a non-issue here because you are combining "man at work" with "capital at work" and it is difficult to measure how much contribution to the profit "man at work" represented. In addition, somewhere during the lifetime of the real estate ownership you will have had to fund negative cash flow because of occupancy and/or expense problems. That is not the point. The real point is that with both real estate and ownership of a closely held business, you are creating capital and converting income to capital at an accelerated rate because of debt paydown, appreciation of property and using leverage effectively.

In the end, you will have an inflation adjusted source of income which is worth far more than the equivalent amount invested in financial assets.

And that is probably the only way you can beat the "taxflation" game if you are relying on a fixed income to provide you with "financial independence."

More money has been made in real estate than in all industrial investments combined.

ANDREW CARNEGIE, 1920

ANNUAL INCREASE IN INCOME
——— 10% ———

AGE	POSITION	ANNUAL INCOME 1991 DOLLARS	ANNUAL INCOME CURRENT DOLLARS @ 6% INFLATION
22	Grad. from College	$ 20,000	$ 20,000
30	Middle Manager	$ 42,871	$ 65,568
38	General Manager	$ 91,897	$ 214,960
45	VP/Corp.	$179,081	$ 607,520
52	Sr. VP/Corp.	$348,978	$1,716,980
62	Ret'd as President	$905,159	$7,574,418

FIGURE #8

EFFECT OF INFLATION ON
INCOME

Income in *2031 Dollars*	**$905,185**

EQUALS

Income in *1991 Dollars*	**$88,003**

FIGURE #9

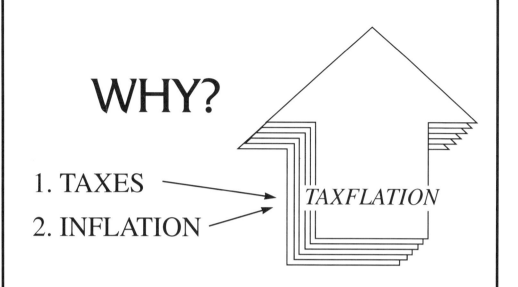

WHY?

1. TAXES
2. INFLATION

TAXFLATION

GROSS INCOME NEEDED TO STAY EVEN WITH INFLATION

TAXES - 33%   –   INFLATION - 6%

YEARS	GROSS SALARY NEEDED
1993 - TODAY	$60,000
1998 - IN 5 YRS.	$102,300
2003 - IN 10 YRS.	$159,600
2008 - IN 15 YRS.	$248,940
2013 - IN 20 YRS.	$388,308

FIGURE #10

Bargain: something you can't use at a price you can't resist.

FRANKLIN P. JONES, 1924

You're worth what you saved, not the millions you made.

JOHN BOYLE O'REILLY, 1878

*It is wonderful to think how men of very large estates not only spend
their yearly income, but are often actually in want of money.*

SAMUEL JOHNSON, 1778

*Remember when people worried about
how much it took to buy something, instead
of how long?*

EARL WILSON, 1962

CHAPTER 14

If you want the good life, why not live it on a discount?

MOST OF US WANT THE BEST THINGS that money can buy. The problem is that in most instances, we want those things precisely at the times we really can't afford them.

I don't mean that we don't necessarily have the money to pay for them, because we might have plenty of income to pay off the debts that those things we buy may create. We might even have the cash in the bank to buy those things outright.

The problem is that at the time we may want those "better" things like a bigger house, a snazzier car or that exotic vacation, we should really be creating capital for our financial independence rather than using that capital for consumables.

Don't worry, the consumables will eventually come, the difference is that we want to be sure it is our capital that is buying them for us and not our income.

Let me illustrate to you how much it really costs us to buy some consumable item prematurely.

Let's say you really want to drive a Mercedez Benz. You can afford the $1,500 per month lease/insurance payment because you are earning well over $100,000 annually and you feel you earned the right to have one. You have paid your dues. The difference between the car you want and a Honda is about $45,000 but, since you are leasing the car, you won't feel the difference, especially since you figure your future raises will pay for it.

To begin with, it really doesn't matter whether you lease the car or whether you pay cash for it. Either way, you have to calculate in the use of money factor. So the $45,000 difference is the same no matter how you have to pay for it.

Well, if you opt for the Honda, in 10 years at 8 percent compounded return, your $45,000 savings will grow to $97,151. In 15 years this difference will be $142,747, and in 20 years it will be $209,743.

That means that within 10 years, just the compounded interest on your savings will be enough to buy you the car at today's prices.

But if at that time you decide to buy it and use your current income to pay off the lease, you will have your car, plus over $200,000 in cash to help you enjoy life when you get close to retirement twenty years from now.

By waiting just a few years, you can have the car and the money to boot.

So the rule in buying expensive consumables is "wait"!

Now, when it comes time for us to actually be purchasing those items, why pay the regular price? Why not create the condition so that the costs related to those items are significantly reduced to us from what we might normally pay for them?

Sounds simple, but in my experience in working with higher income/higher net worth families, I found how little of this is really being done.

When we want something, we go out and buy it. That's it! Regardless of the price of the item at the time.

As a matter of fact, I found that some people actually feel embarrassed about shopping in discount places as if to say that it is demeaning to their status.

They will prefer to pay double and triple in designer boutiques rather than rummage for bargains in Filene's basement or making a visit to Wal Mart or the Shopping Club.

Let me put this whole discount shopping idea for you in perspective.

If you want to buy a Brooks Brother's suit, and actually go to Brooks Brothers on Madison Ave., you can probably expect to pay $800 or $1,000 for a good one.

On the other hand, if you go to Daffy Dan's in New York, or

Filene's basement in Boston, you will probably pay $200 to $300 for that same suit.

If you are looking at Brooks Brothers suits to begin with, you are probably in the top income tax bracket, which means that by the time you get done paying state and city income taxes, at least 40 percent of your income will go to the government.

For most of us, the purchase of suits is not a tax deductible event, therefore we do this with after tax dollars. What that means is that for us to pay regular price for this suit we have to soak up about $1,700 of our earned income. On the other hand, if we buy this same suit at a discount, it will only take about $500 of that earned income.

Now, let's suppose that our gross earned income is $150,000 annually. To pay full price, we use over 1 percent of that gross income just to buy the suit. If we buy at a discount, we spend only one-third of one percent of our income to accomplish the same thing.

Now let's look at it another way. Let's say that 85 percent of our gross income is spoken for to pay our taxes, our basic living expenses and our housing. That leaves us 15% or $22,500 for discretionary purchases which may include clothing. That means that we soak up almost 8 percent of that discretionary income for the suit if we pay full price and if we buy at a discount, we only use little over 2 percent to accomplish the same thing.

One more quick look at the effect of shopping for a discount.

If we were to place this difference of $1,200 between the regular cost of this suit and what we would pay at a discount into some tax-sheltered savings program, and assuming we are 35 years old, by the time we retire, this difference, at average return of 8 percent will grow to over $12,000.

It may not sound like much, but you probably shop for clothing every year, so if you repeat this twenty or thirty times during your working lifetime, you are probably looking at a cool quarter of a million dollars of savings.

And the best part is that you are still really wearing the same suit. It may not be the exact latest cut, but essentially, it is the same suit.

Is it worth it? You be the judge!

But shopping for clothes at a discount is not the only place where you should be looking for a bargain. When shopping for household accessories, why not buy as many things as possible in a store like Wal-Mart?

When I was furnishing my house in Vail, I will never forget my first trip to buy accessories to Wal Mart stores. I came out with a couple of shopping carts overflowing with bags full of "good junk" and the price tag came to $280.

There were a couple of items that I still needed and I had to buy them in a regular store. I paid close to $100 for those items. A tiny little bag. I cried when I paid that bill.

You can also get similar discounts on food, carpeting, drapes, automobiles, furniture, art, jewelry, cosmetics, just to name a few items. All you have to do is make an effort to look and you will wind up saving thousands upon thousands of after tax dollars each year which you can use to enhance your financial independence.

But for some reason most of us insist on overpaying for the purchases we make. I believe this is a total ego trip. Somehow, once we reach a certain economic "status" we find it embarrassing to shop for discounts. We feel it is somehow demeaning to look for a bargain. We consider ourselves above negotiating a good deal.

We get hooked on being taken to the cleaners in fancy boutiques and feel superior by being able to pay full price and then some for the things we buy. And we do this while we charge those items to our Visa and Master Cards.

Once, I went on a Safari in Kenya. It was an incredible trip and I would highly recommend it to anyone. The trip included a couple of weeks in three different game preserves, stays at lodges, meals, transfers along with first class air fare.

It was truly a superb experience. During this trip I met a couple from New England. They were in their mid-fifties and he was an executive for a major corporation.

Judging by where they lived and the kinds of things they did, and me being in the business of Personal Finance, I guessed to myself that they probably had a seven-figure net worth and that his income was probably in the multiple six-figure category.

We became friendly and spent some very nice moments together.

Everything was fine until the conversation came around to what I did. Not wanting to get into a business discussion which always happens when I tell people that I am in the investment advisory business, I decided to tell them only about a business which I happen to own but which is managed by a full-time manager. A travel agency called Travel With Jane.

Immediately I was labeled in their mind as a "lowly" travel agent, who no longer was worthy to associate with the "elite" who paid thousands of dollars for their trip while mine only cost me $700 and which was tax deductible to me because it was, based on tax rules considered a "fam trip". (In the travel industry a "Fam Trip" means familiarization with a travel destination and therefore, based on tax rules is a legimate business activity.)

We stayed in the same hotels, ate the same food, drank the same wine, even took pictures of the same animals, yet somehow, a difference was created because we did not pay the same price for this same experience.

This, I believe is the crux of what I call the "elitist syndrome" which somehow infects people once they reach certain economic levels and which, I believe, keeps those who come down with this illness, constantly broke.

Somehow, when you reach a certain level in the pecking order, you are judged not necessarily by who you are but by what you spend. And the more you overspend, the more respected you become in the eyes of other overspenders. Therefore, by looking for a discount, you are really undermining your prestige among your overspender peers.

If I had actually spent $8000 or $10,000 for my trip as did most of the people who were there, then I would have been part of this little overspender club. But, by being smart enough not to spend that amount of money to enjoy the same things that everybody else was enjoying and making my insignificant cost tax deductible to boot, that made me an outcast.

Somehow being smarter, in this case, didn't mean praise and respect, it meant contempt.

I know, had I told them the whole story, that I really no longer needed to earn a living by the time I was in my mid-forties and that I only worked six months out of the year, this probably would have spoiled their vacation.

I didn't want to go that far, so I preferred to remain just a poor travel agent in their minds so that they could preserve the security of the cocoon they had woven for themselves.

So living on a discount does have its price. Your ego will not have the same heyday as if you were just another overspender.

Now, I ask you, is this ego trip really worth the price of juggling your checkbook? Not to me it isn't, and for that reason I don't hesitate to tell anyone who is willing to listen that no matter what you buy, you should be paying less than the original asking retail price. If you don't, you are just throwing your money away. And for what? Because you are embarrassed to haggle and bargain and look for the best deal?

The most ridiculous excuse I ever heard for not trying to get the best price for some item was: "I am not made this way!"

This is as if to say that those people who would walk into a shoe store and ask for an extra five dollars off just for the hell of it are somehow lesser people that those that don't.

That's ridiculous. Every businessman's objective is to transfer as much as possible of your money, as the consumer, into his pocket.

And it should be your objective, as the consumer, that he should wind up with as little of your money as possible.

This process to me is beautiful. It is the epitome of free enterprise. Isn't it wonderful to have the ability to set your own price based on your skill as a bargainer rather than some government dictating to you how much you should pay for something?

And yet we, in America, the bastion of free enterprise, are embarrassed to ask the guy who is selling us a shirt to knock off another five bucks from the ticket price.

When I was in Chicago, visiting my son, and we went shopping at the Lord and Taylor discount outlet, we saw a designer jacket that was ripped a little bit next to the buttons on the sleeve. It fit my son beautifully and it's regular price was $395 which they had marked down to $150.

I asked to speak to the store manager and showed him the rip on the sleeve and suggested that the reason he probably will never sell this jacket was because of this rip. I offered him $15 for the jacket. He took it gladly. It cost my son five bucks to sew on a button which easily hid the tear underneath it.

You know what my son said while I was going through this process? "Oh, Dad, how could you? This is embarrassing!" You know something; that's his favorite jacket now.

What a great country! God bless America!

*It requires a great deal of boldness and a great deal of caution
to make a fortune, and when you have it, it requires
ten times as much wit to keep it.*

MEYER ROTHSCHILD, c. 1830

*There was a time when a fool and his money were soon parted,
but now it happens to everybody.*

ADLAI STEVENSON, 1966

On the soft beds of luxury most kingdoms have expired.

EDWARD YOUNG, 1725

If money is your hope for independence you will never have it. The only real security that a man can have in this world is a reserve of knowledge, experience and ability.

HENRY FORD, 1926

CHAPTER 15

Protecting your capital / Using insurance and the law

WHAT WE STILL NEED TO DISCUSS is how we can actually protect our income and our capital from the forces that take it away and the methods we have available to make sure we get to keep what we have worked hard to accumulate. What I am talking about here is Insurance with a capital "I."

Your first reaction might be: "Okay I've got life insurance, health insurance, disability insurance, property insurance and liability insurance. What else do I need?"

It is absolutely true that you need all of the above coverage because you need to protect your income in case of death and disability, you need to have some kind of plan that will pay for your medical costs if you get sick, and you need to have hazard insurance in case your house burns down and, if somebody sues you because of some property you own or a profession you practice, you need to have enough money for legal fees and to pay off whoever sues you in case you lose the case.

But carrying all that coverage is just not enough. There are many situations that fall through the cracks of insurance protection, and unless you know how to recover your losses from them, they will wipe you out just as quickly as you can blink your eye.

Let's first talk about your income. This is probably your most valuable asset that you possess.

Previously, we talked about a young man graduating from college at age 22, getting a job paying him $20,000 per year, and 40 years later, at age 62, retiring as president of the company. We assumed that his salary would increase at a rate of 10 percent per year.

Well, during his working years, he would have earned close to ten million dollars. That means that regardless of his ability to invest his money, just his capacity to earn an income over that period would be worth the ten million dollars.

Your ability to earn an income is what will create capital for you, and will pay your living expenses. If your income stops because of an accident or illness, unless you have coverage that will protect you, you will eat up whatever capital you have accumulated to pay those living expenses.

But accident or illness is not the only thing that can prevent you from earning a living. You can lose your job for many reasons, and your ability to earn an income in the future could be impaired because you lost your job.

If you feel that you have been terminated wrongfully you may have recourse via a lawsuit against your employer. You have every right to recover the capital you would lose if you feel your employer has done something illegal or improper when he fired you.

The problem is that most people are reluctant to file a lawsuit against their employer because they still feel some sort of loyalty. Or they may fear that if they did file the lawsuit, they may not be able to find another job in that field.

The important thing to remember is that the only loyalty you should have is to yourself and your family. And that you have every right to recover whatever capital you might have lost if your employer suddenly decided to let you go for what you may feel is an unjust reason.

Remember, you gave your employer your time, your productivity and years of your life. If the company is suddenly reducing its work force because their profits are down, and this effects you negatively, you have a right to know why you are being let go and not someone else.

In a previous chapter, I talked briefly about my career in the insurance business. When I came back to Puerto Rico, I came back as General Agent in Puerto Rico for the the company I represented previously. As a General Agent I had certain elements of ownership, whereas an Agency Manager is strictly an employee of the company who manages a company branch office.

Without getting into any more detail about those two relationships, during the early eighties, my company decided to change its system of operation from "General Agency" to "Branch Office" which would be headed by an agency manager, and I was given the job.

They offered certain financial inducements to all the General Agents for making the switch. From my viewpoint, those financial inducements were not enough. The fact was, we had no choice. The decision was made by corporate executives who were not necessarily thinking about my well being but instead that of the company and, perhaps, their own. And my financial future hung on that decision.

There were about 150 General Agents nationwide that were effected by this decision. In most instances, those of us who were effected, lost capital.

The fact that the insurance company I represented was probably as good an insurance company to be affiliated with as one could find had nothing to do with the problem. The problem was I had counted on one type of system of operation and, after putting my efforts into this system, was told that I would have to function under a different system which would take away some of my capital.

Just as there was nothing personal about the company's decision to change the system, there was also nothing personal in the fact I decided to file a lawsuit against the company. Their decision to take my capital was no different than my decision to get it back. What surprised me was there were only about a handful of other General Agents that did the same thing. When I talked to some of the others who did not sue the company, their responses were: "The company has been good to me for so many years and I don't want to appear disloyal;" "If I sue them, I will probably not be able to find another job in the insurance industry of a comparable level because they will blackball me in the industry;" "I have friends in high places and if I sued the company I may hurt them;" "If I file a lawsuit and lose, I will have wasted a lot of time and energy;" "I don't want to appear like a trouble maker."

If you notice, all the responses were emotional and centered around fear and false loyalties.

To my way of thinking, if my company wasn't loyal enough to me to keep me on the same system that I had enjoyed operating on, then why should I be loyal to them while they reach into my pocket and take away my capital?

These fears and false loyalties on the part of the other General Agents wound up costing those who opted not to sue a big chunk of their capital. In the meantime, since most General Agents opted not to sue, the insurance company was able to add many millions of dollars to their profits.

I have no hard feelings whatsoever in this case. The company I represented is a fine company, and it made a good business decision (for them) to change the system. On the other hand, I made a good business decision (for me) to sue them and eventually (it took me over six years) I collected my money.

And the General Agents who opted not to sue? They are probably still working while I am skiing.

The point of the matter is that many times, and perhaps for good business reasons, your employer may decide to change your employment status that may effect you negatively. There is nothing personal in that decision. It is strictly business!

He has every right to make that decision and if he does it properly, well, such is life! However, if you feel the action was improper, you should also take the same attitude, and seek recourse. Nothing personal, strictly business! And don't allow emotions like false loyalties and fear from making your "strictly business" decision.

It's your capital and if it reflects itself in corporate dividends instead of your bank account, it is purely your fault.

I love the insurance company I represented for what I was able to accomplish while I was with them. However, I also love the fact that my money is in my bank account and not some stockholder's pocket.

Once again, creation of capital can be reduced to a simple shift in attitude. And many times, our attitudes are swayed by misguided emotions and false loyalties. To come out ahead, we have to keep our heads clear and keep emotions out of those decisions that effect our capital. Strictly business!

Another area where we miss the boat and wind up losing some of our capital, is in the area of insurance purchases and insurance claims.

It is important that we insure, as much as possible, all our exposures to hazards.

The first step in the process is to be sure we are dealing with the right agent.

When you are buying policies, fancy proposals and flowery promises of eternal service and bliss may sweep you off your feet. But when it comes time to collect, if you've picked the wrong agent, you may wind up with too little, too late.

An early indicator of whether your insurance agent is working for you or just collecting commissions is at policy renewal time. If all you get is a renewal bill, you should begin to get suspicious.

A good agent will offer to review your coverage at renewal time and attempt to place your property and casualty insurance with the most competitive carrier. A poor one will send you a bill and then send you a cancellation notice if you don't pay it on time.

Sometimes, fires, floods, hurricanes, or earthquakes can wipe out a lifetime of capital accumulated with your sweat. And your recovery of this capital depends on how well you can negotiate your claim with the insurance company.

When you incur a claim, this is an opportunity for your agent to really shine. If he is working in your best interest, he or she will review your coverage, compare them to your losses and try to maximize the amount of dollars you collect from the insurance company. He will intervene on your behalf with the adjustor and help you collect everything you are entitled to collect.

Remember, the insurance company adjustor is not on your side. His job is to "adjust" which often means reducing the claim you are making. As a matter of fact, the adjustor makes his living in direct proportion to how much he can reduce your claim. Your agent, if he is good, will call the adjustor's bluff and insist that your claim gets the full payment it deserves.

For example, if your couch burns down in a fire and it needs to be replaced, and you go shopping for a comparable couch and find one on sale at 50 percent off, the claim to the insurance company should be for the full price of the couch and not for it's discounted cost. If you are able to find a bargain, there is nothing in your insurance company contract that says you must pass those savings on to the insurance company. Those savings are due to you because you happen to be an astute shopper.

What is interesting to note is that insurance companies charge extra premiums on all their policies because they anticipate that claims will be exaggerated. That means you are paying the premium for the right to exaggerate your claim. Whether you want to take advantage of this fact is entirely up to you, but you are paying for this special extra privilege.

Many insurance companies, in order to keep the agent on their side of the negotiations, many times pay agents what is called a "quality bonus."

This bonus is based on what insurance companies call "loss ratios." Here is how it works: If an agent collects $1 million in premiums and his clients receive $500,000 in claims, he has a 50 percent loss ratio on his book of business for that year. The next year, the company may offer him a bonus of say $25,000. if he were able to reduce this ratio to 40 percent.

That means it is in the agent's best interest to have you collect as little as possible on your claim.

You immediately will know if the agent is working for you or for his "quality bonus" by what he says to you when you make the claim. If he begins to say things like: "Let's not be greedy on this claim," or "Let's make the claim fair and try to salvage as much as we can," that means he is taking money out of your pocket to place it into his.

The agent may be appealing to your sense of guilt, fear or "fair play" in order to line his own pocket. If those are the signals you are getting, get yourself another agent as soon as your policies come up for renewal.

Remember, you are paying the premiums and you are entitled to everything the policy says. If that means you make a profit on your claim, don't feel guilty. You paid for it!

If the insurance company adjustor gives you a hard time, don't accept it. Write to the Commissioner of Insurance and file a complaint. And don't be afraid to take the case to your attorney if you feel you are not getting what you are entitled to.

In some instances, it may be smart to hire your own public adjustor who will work for you and try to squeeze as much out of the insurance company as possible. A public adjustor normally charges a percentage of what he collects for you and, in most cases, is worth every penny.

But insurance cannot cover you in case of all contingencies. You can still be subject to a lawsuit if you managed to beat off the forces that kept you away from accumulating a sizeable net worth and are now in the position of being the deep pocket.

Circumstances beyond your control could cause your business to go bankrupt, or if you are a professional, your liability policy may have gaps that may leave you exposed.

Or anybody who feels they may have some recourse against you may decide to sue you. And a lawsuit, win lose or draw, could wipe most people out.

Remember, just like you have a right to sue if you feel someone has taken your capital wrongfully, you also can be the subject of a lawsuit by someone who may feel the same way about you. Especially if you happen to have made a "strictly business" decision that enhanced your financial position but perhaps at the expense of someone else.

There are many ways to protect yourself from unexpected lawsuits. One of those ways is by setting up what is called an "Asset Protection Trust." Here is how it works:

To protect yourself, you can set up a limited partnership with you being the General Partner and place much of your assets into this partnership. As General Partner you would own 1 percent of the assets of this partnership and the other 99 percent of the assets would be owned by the limited partners. The Limited Partnership shares would be owned by a trust for the benefit of your children which you create outside of the U.S.

As General Partner, you have full control of the assets and you can use them any way you want.

If someone sues you or you need to declare bankruptcy, the assets held in the partnership cannot be attached because they technically do not belong to you.

Since most plaintiff attorneys work on a contingency basis, they will be discouraged from taking the case against you because in order to collect from you they will have to sue you in some exotic foreign jurisdiction which may not be too receptive to their lawsuit.

And even though the trust is offshore, your assets could be in the good old U.S.A. or anywhere in the world that you may chose them to be.

The theory here is that since the attorney of the individual who is suing you is working on a contingency basis, he would be reluctant to take on the case if in the end the chances of him collecting his fee would be slim to none.

Before you embark on such a program, however, make sure you consult with your attorney. But most important of all, make sure that your attorney has had sufficient experience in the areas of estate planning and trusts - especially foreign or offshore trusts.

Once again, your attitude will determine whether you are going to recover or get to keep your capital if someone makes a decision to take it away from you.

And unless you place yourself in a defensive position, you will have worked hard so that someone else can enjoy your money.

It is not the man who has little, but he who desires more, that is poor.

SENECA, C. A.D. 40

*Avarice, or the desire of gain, is a universal passion, which operates
at all times, at all places, and upon all persons.*

DAVID HUME, 1754

If you wish to remove avarice you must remove its mother, luxury.

CICERO, C 46 B.C.

Perpetual devotion to what a man calls his business, is only to be sustained by perpetual neglect of many other things.

ROBERT LOUIS STEVENSON, 1881

CHAPTER 16

Relationships, marriage and divorce / doing it right!

WHEN YOU GET MARRIED, chances are better than 50/50 you will get divorced. And divorce is one of the biggest "capital killers."

Many a fortune has been dissipated because of ugly litigation that usually results from a bitterly disputed divorce.

But the conversion of capital into legal fees is not the only by product of such a divorce. In most cases, the children are the ones that ultimately wind up paying the biggest price.

The problem begins when a marriage, which might have actually ended years before, continues as a Mexican standoff, with each spouse barely tolerating each other, but staying together for some unrelated reason like "the children" or "for economic reasons" or because of "the house".

Those of you who have seen the movie: "The War of the Roses," have witnessed this type of destructive reasoning unfold and take hold of two what seem to be well adjusted and intelligent people, turning them into monsters. At least to each other.

This state of affairs eventually turns rancorous because each spouse begins to feel robbed of their youthful years and as a result, begins to do things deliberately to "get even" with the other spouse during this miserable living-together stage.

Each spouse seems to look for excuses to make it look like it is the "other person's fault" so that they absolve themselves of any guilt that might come from the inevitable breakup.

When the break eventually comes, sometimes after many wasted years of living in total misery, the pent up bitter feelings explode and the lawyers walk in and the roulette wheel starts to spin. Your financial life hangs on the chance of which judge will handle your case and who represents you and your spouse.

I have personally seen situations where the wife kept all the assets, and the husband wound up with all the debts, with his income tied up for years in alimony and child support payments. In one situation, the husband wound up with less than one third of his gross income. He hardly had enough money left for gas to drive to work.

Here is another horror story. I saw a successful surgeon, driving a spiffy foreign car, while his children barely had enough to eat and his ex-wife worked two jobs just to make ends meet. Her spare time was spent baking cakes that she sold for extra money.

How could this surgeon, earning hundreds of thousands of dollars a year, wind up paying just a few hundred dollars per month for child support for his three kids? What was the judge smoking when he made that decision?

Of course, not all court decisions are that unfair. But the fact is when you make the decision to get divorced and there is a dispute, you will be faced with the most unfair process I have ever seen.

The outcome is totally dependent on who your lawyer is, who your spouse's lawyer is, and who the judge is. It is a total crap shoot and if you take this road, chances are both you and your spouse will wind up in the poor house and your children will be the real victims.

The divorce process usually begins when either one of the couples finally has had enough of the pretense of the "marriage" and, on the advice of his or her friends, goes to see an attorney for the divorce.

The attorney immediately takes the attitude of "Let's see how much we can get out of this," and proceeds to advise the client how to best maximize the financial outcome of the divorce for his client.

The other spouse is by no means asleep at the switch. He or she goes to their attorney who in turn advise them of the same thing.

Now we have two attorneys advising their clients how to best take their spouse to the cleaners.

Sometimes the process really gets dirty, where each spouse begins to hide and camouflage assets so that it appears that the total estate is either bigger or smaller than what it really is.

Each side begin lying to the other. In the meantime, the children see all this going on, maybe even get dragged into court. They get confused, hurt and perhaps affected by this debacle for the rest of their lives.

In the meantime, the billable time clock is running, and the fees are piling up. Some attorneys fees are based not just on their regular hourly fees but also represent a percentage of the amount of money that they can gouge out of the other spouse.

Talk about an adversary situation? This is a total "lose/lose" situation with no winner!

How can two intelligent human beings be so blind and use this type of a system to end what might be a bad marriage now, but at one time must have given them some happiness and good times. Especially if the marriage has given them the greatest gift that we can ever hope for in our lives - our children.

To my way of thinking, this is the most ridiculous way of ending narriage. It is totally destructive for all the parties concerned.

So how do we avoid this kind of debacle?

To begin with, it is important not to hang on to your losses. It is most important to recognize when the marriage is over and to sit down and talk sensibly with your spouse and state this fact plainly and honestly.

No games! Just: "This isn't working out and I think we should end it."

If the marriage is over, end it formally before the hate and the resentment makes it impossible to part as friends. This way, children won't feel abandoned. They won't witness the anger that normally precedes and follows a divorce. And they will feel secure that it is not "their fault" that their parents are getting divorced.

This is tough to do, but if you really mean that you are willing to "sacrifice because of the children," you better do it just that way. Hanging on to the marriage for dear life is worse for them than ending the marriage amicably sooner.

You have got to put your children's needs above your own in this case.

The next step is to sit down and discuss the financial consequences of the divorce. That is what most of the legal fight is all about.

So why not end this legal fight before it even begins.

Figure out between the two of you how you should split up the assets and discuss the child support arrangements. If you really love your children as you say you do, you will compromise.

Eventually you will need a lawyer to formalize the divorce.

Do not, and I repeat, do not each of you find yourself a divorce lawyer to accomplish this. This type of lawyer will fuel the fires of dispute.

Find yourself a good corporate "contract" lawyer, and ask him or her to act as your "referee." The reason I specify corporate contract lawyer is because this type of lawyer has had a lot of experience dealing in AGREEMENTS and not DISAGREEMENTS as would have had a divorce attorney. He knows that the elements of any good contract are that it must be fair to both parties. No contract works unless either party can stand on each side of the fence and feel that it is a good agreement.

Initially, this attorney's response will be "I don't do divorces," but when you explain to him or her what you are hiring them to do, I believe they will be delighted to help you in this case. And if he doesn't want to handle the actual legal filing of the divorce, authorize him to use someone else on a sub-contract basis.

If it looks like you might have a dispute about either property division or income, ask your attorney what he feels is fair.

If that answer does not satisfy you, then hire yourself a mediator, who will help bring the two of you together in your thinking. These people are very effective and they are not very expensive.

One thing will happen during this process. For some unexplained reason, an attorney who happens to be handling "both sides" as in this case, has a duty to recommend to you that once you have reached an agreement, that you should each then get your own attorney to review this agreement. If you do that, you will be risking everything that you have accomplished during this process.

If you love your children, do not follow this particular brand of advice. You see, as soon as you go to "your own" attorney, he or she will feel it a duty to protect you and get for you as much as possible. That means that you will get recommendations from him that would make your position more favorable to you. That is when the adversarial relationship begins. Use your good judgement to make "your deal," but don't allow outside influences to destroy the relationship that you may still have left with your ex-spouse.

Remember, you did have some good feelings for each other when you got married. Some of them may still exist. Don't throw out the baby with the bathwater.

Believe me, especially when children are involved, a couple of extra dollars one way or another is not worth the wear and tear on your children's mental well being.

While you are going through this process, remember, you are divorcing your spouse and not your children. Therefore you need to be committed to this type of divorce process, and not the typical "cat fight."

Therefore you need to be flexible in your agreements.

Of course, this scenario assumes that neither spouse is ready for the straight jacket, and that each is responsible and mature enough to put the children's interests above their own immediate desire to inflict pain on the other.

If you go through this process successfully, you will wind up saving a bundle in legal fees and much of your estate will remain intact.

And if this idea doesn't work, there is still the traditional way of getting divorced.

Hire the most aggressive attorneys you can find and send them into court with combat armor and assault weapons blazing. Remember however, that the stray bullets will probably not be hitting your spouse. Chances are they will be headed straight for your children.

How much money are they worth to you?

If you were able to successfully accomplish the separation of your marriage amicably, there is an excellent chance that you will be in for a pleasant surprise.

When you originally married your now ex-spouse, it was probably because he or she had some qualities that you liked. Chances are that those qualities are still present. Perhaps the marriage may be over, but that doesn't necessarily mean that the friendship has to be over, too. You'd be surprised how great it is for the kids when they see their mother and father making the effort to still raise them together as friends and not as enemies.

Perhaps the Bar Associations in this country will not be very happy with what I am recommending, but believe me, your children will be. And they are the ones that count.

So in this case, regardless of what the Bar Association may think of me, I highly recommend that you do not follow your attorney's advice but follow your conscience instead.

So far, what I have talked about in this chapter is the traditional type of divorce from a traditional type marriage.

But many relationships don't necessarily fall into this "traditional" category. To begin with, when you make the decision to go though the legal process of getting married, you are bringing into the relationship many legal parameters and societal rules that have nothing to do with your particular relationship.

By "officially" getting married, you are suddenly expected to respect a lot of rules that are not yours or your partner's but those of strangers attempting to impose their standards on you through various laws relating to marriage and divorce.

For the above reason, many people prefer to let their own conscience guide them on the rules for their relationship instead of having someone else make those decisions for them.

Relationships are tough enough to maintain, without having the added pressure of other people's opinions infringing on your privacy and your freedown.

Many people, however, turn to a "formal" marriage because to them it may represent both financial and emotional security. They feel that because of those outside rules, they will somehow be protected.

But one does not have to take on a whole set of irrelevant criteria for a relationship if all they want is a little security.

I believe a much wiser approach to this security question would be to sit down and specifically discuss with your partner what you expect from them during the relationship and, in the event the relationship turns sour, what you expect at the break up.

I know it is difficult to discuss this potential breakup at a time that you are in love, but since more than 50 percent of marriages wind up in divorce, chances are you will probably be discussing this breakup under a lot more unpleasant circumstances sooner or later. Why not do it now while you are both in a positive and constructive frame of mind rather than when you are at each other's throats?

Why not spell out on paper what you expect from each other while you are together and what you want from each other in case of a breakup?

You can address the handling of personal finances while you are together, division of property, in case of a breakup, income to either partner if one partner gave up a career to be with the other, and income to support children, along with custody questions, if eventually there are children.

All these ideas can be discussed, reduced to writing and can become legally binding. A simple contract can be drafted as to how all personal finances should be handled during the relationship and after a breakup.

The most important positive effect of such discussions is that each partner will feel secure in knowing what the expectations of the other happen to be. I believe if there are no ulterior motives for the relationship, it should help cement the couple in their trust in each other If there are ulterior motives, they will come out and each partner will have an opportunity to decide what they are willing to give up in order to gain what they really want out of this relationship.

Once this agreement is in place, if both partners feel that a "formal" marriage will represent a more positive impact on raising the children or for other personal reasons, then the couple could legally get married and their agreement could be made to take precedence over many of the rules that normally govern a formal marriage and divorce.

This type of agreement is pretty much the rule when two partners go into business. It is called a "Partnership and Buy/Sell Agreement." Why shouldn't it also become a rule when two people decide to commit to a personal relationship? Anyone who goes into business with another person without such an agreement is at best naive and at worst a fool. Why not start a personal partnership right, where all the expectations are on the table?

We Americans worship the almighty dollar!
Well, it is a worthier god than Heredity Privilege.

MARK TWAIN, 1894

The trick is to make sure you don't die waiting for prosperity to come.

LEE A. IACOCCA, 1973

Happiness seems to require a modicum of external prosperity.

ARISTOTLE, c 360 B.C.

*Can anybody remember where the times
were not hard, and money not scarce?*

RALPH WALDO EMERSON, 1870

CHAPTER 17

Wealth, life, and making it / A personal perspective

Wealth is Relative:

ATTAINING FINANCIAL INDEPENDENCE is a function of attitude because it is more of a state of mind than an actual measure of someone's net worth. It is completely dependent on one's values and one's definition of "needs," therefore it is not absolute. It is relative.

For example, recently, on a T.V. program I saw Robert Maxwell's apartment with all it's contents being auctioned off just to pay his back bills. This was someone who was considered, while he was alive, one of the wealthiest people in the world.

Yet it appears that his "wealth" seemed to have existed as long as he was personally driving his businesses. That is "man at work."

As soon as he died, his "empire" collapsed and based on news media reports, there were more debts than assets. In other words there was not enough "capital at work" there to sustain his expenses once he stopped producing income. For all his toys, he didn't really achieve financial independence.

This was an extreme case, of course, and most people who do reach the level of success in business that he did would have enough capital to sustain their standard of living for an indefinite period of time.

With Robert Maxwell as an example of an extreme case on one side of the spectrum, let's now take a close look at another equally extreme case that falls on the opposite side of the spectrum.

I am using the following story to illustrate how we, who live in a middle class world, are so far removed not only from Mr. Maxwell's super rich world but even more so from the dark and miserable world of the super poor. And that only we can define wealth as it applies to us and no one else.

Sometime ago, while I was riding my bicycle, I rode past a homeless person lounging under the shade of a large palm tree, enjoying the view of the lagoon and reading a magazine.

I was curious to see what he was reading, and as I stopped and inched closer, I caught a glimpse of the title page. It was Business Week!

At first I thought I had mistaken a resident from one of the surrounding condominiums for a street bum.

As I looked closer, however, I saw the unmistakable signs: dirty fingernails, disheveled hair, ripped pants, growth of beard, a smell that could knock you over and, of course, the Business Week Magazine.

For the next few hours I agonized over the meaning behind the scene I had just witnessed.

Finally I came to the conclusion that there is a whole world of people out there who most of us living in comfortable little cocoons and driving to work in snazzy foreign machines, know nothing about.

In retrospect, I wish I'd had the presence of mind to stop and ask the man who he was, where he was from, and how he became a street person.

Most of all, I wish I'd asked him what possible reason he might have for staying current with world economic trends.

Unfortunately, I succumbed to the "I don't want to know" syndrome, probably for the same reason that most of us who live in protected little cocoons would.

If I had stopped and asked, would he have asked me for money? Or threatened me with a knife or a gun and robbed me?

Or was I afraid he might tell me that just a few years ago he, too, lived in a comfortable little cocoon until something happened to change his life. Could that same thing happen to me?

Was I afraid to find out that someone who from my perspective, appeared to be a wretched human being was actually very much like me in many respects?

Or was my real fear that, after talking to him, I might discover that the effort and stress needed to create and protect our little cocoons may not be worth the trouble?

In the end we all wind up in the same place regardless of whether we spent our lives as a street bum or an upstanding member of our community.

As I struggled with these thoughts, the words of a song by Janice Joplin, the famous 1960's rock singer, came to my mind: "Freedom is another word for nothing left to lose."

Then the real question hit me: Did this street bum know something I didn't? Did he discover the true answer to Life's happiness by rejecting all material possessions and deciding to spend his life without the burdens of wealth?

And in doing so did he discover the true meaning of "Financial Independence"?

And what's wrong with that? A couple of thousand years ago a middle class carpenter came to the same conclusion, and decided to dump his material possessions and tell his story to the world. And look what happened.

We can philosophize on that one ad infinitum, but the real point of the story is that here we have on one side of the spectrum, one of the "wealthiest" people in the world who obviously did not achieve financial independence and on the other side, we have someone who has nothing, yet who perhaps has everything he needs materially.

Could it mean that to this hobo, who still reads Business Week and seems to be in tune with the material world, ego needs are meaningless? Whereas to Robert Maxwell, with the high-spending pattern, ego must have been a strong driving force, and because of that he may not have been as happy as he appeared on the surface.

These assumptions may sound preposterous, but food for thought never the less.

As we have explored in other chapters, attitude, perspective and individual values are everything, while toys and outside appearances and trappings are nothing more than fodder for our egos. They have no relationship.

Happiness is Living in Your World and Not Someone Else's:

An American who can make money, invoke God, and be no better than his neighbor, has nothing to fear but truth itself.

MARYA MANNES, 1958

It took me a while to learn that overcoming prejudice and discrimination so that I could achieve my potential, can only be done in a world I created for myself. When I first came to Canada in my early teens, a different message was drummed into my head.

I don't know how many of you have experienced prejudice, but for those who have, this story will most likely hit home.

Canada and the U.S., even though they are a conglomeration of numerous cultures and races are by no means a "melting pot".

Essentially, they are a male dominated "club" of the ethnic groups that happen to be in control of a specific segment of industry or government or piece of geography at a particular period in time. They happen to tolerate other nationalities, races and religions, when it is convenient for them to do so but essentially, if you want to get ahead in the "club," you better be one of them.

As a nonmember of the "club," you have to work twice as hard, produce twice as much, and be twice as bright as "them" in order to be recognized.

And in many instances, no matter how good or qualified you happen to be, you can never expect to get certain privileges and recognitions.

If you don't believe me, tell me how many Blacks, Hispanics, Females, Orientals, Jews, Indians and Immigrants in general do you see running the government or our nation's large corporations?

To be sure, there are some, but most of those who are have had to create their own world by either being elected by mostly their own kind or by placing themselves in a position of control to take the position that they wanted. Very seldom is a position "awarded" by "them" to "non-them" because of pure merit!

When I was in the insurance and securities business, no one ever "promoted" me to something. The only reason I was able to reach the various positions that I did was because someone higher than me in the pecking order had something to gain by making me the offer. In other words, I did not get something because I was qualified. I got it because somebody profited more by placing me there than he might have profited from placing someone else there.

But, such is life in the big city!

Now don't get me wrong. I am not knocking the system. It did fine by me once I learned how to work within it. As a matter of fact, there are few systems in this world that are as easy to penetrate as this one, and prejudice is a way of life no matter where you happen to go in this world.

The problem is that most people naively believe in the fallacy of "freedom and equality for all." According to a famous Boston University historian, Howard Zinn, when the Constitution was originally written, the freedoms it talked about specifically excluded blacks, Indians, women and indentured servants. It was reserved for the "privileged class" or members of the "club" if you will.

Think of it this way, the Constitution and the Bill of Rights were written at a time when this country had hundreds of thousands human beings in slavery. Does that make the document, the greatest example of hypocrisy ever produced? I may not be qualified to make that judgement, but what do you think?

Yet it is this very same attitude that makes this country probably the only place in this world where anyone can give birth to an idea in their own mind, then convert this idea to a reality by simply acting it out. What I am saying is that this hypocrisy really exemplifies the right of an individual to invent and then implement a narrow viewpoint knowing that he or she will be respected for doing so not necessarily because this viewpoint is correct and truthful but simply because everyone else knows that they, too, have the right to do the same thing.

That to me is what the essence of what the constitution exemplifies. It is not the words, but it is the concept of our undenyable right to be a hypocrite, if we so chose to be.

Because of this, we may not be able to win a world popularity contest, but we are respected.

We have the right to believe our own bull, but we don't necessarily have to believe everybody else's.

The problem is that most people take this "equality" business literally, and when it doesn't work in their case because they are not in the club, they feel that they have been cheated and feel sorry for themselves. What they don't understand is that there are those with privilege and then there are those without privilege. If you are without privilege, you have to make your own world and march to your own drummer and create your own privilege. But before you start, you have to understand who and what you are, otherwise you will be beating your head against the wall.

Anyway, here I was in Toronto, Canada on my first day in school. I was seated in the front of the class and the teacher was speaking in what to me was a weird language, English, of which I understood nothing.

Every once in a while the teacher would ask me a question and, since I didn't understand a word she was saying, I would just shrug my shoulders. The teacher's response was to hit me over the head with a book. Perhaps the teacher's perception of learning and teaching was to physically force the contents of a book filled with English words into the cranium of a student. But I wasn't going to argue with that concept even if I could. Anything outside of a DP camp was a step in the right direction for me.

But I also realized that this kind of system could not continue indefinitely.

So I decided to take some positive steps to prevent it. I knew that the first thing I had to do was to communicate with someone who might teach me what was really going on here.

I tried talking to some of the other students in Russian, Serbo Croatian and Italian (which I had picked up in DP camps) but to no avail. Everybody spoke only English.

I then noticed a little dark looking kid sitting in the row next to me who I felt certain looked Italian.

I approached him in Italian but he just shrugged his shoulders and walked away. This was very frustrating for me because I could feel in my bones that he was Italian.

I then decided to take some physical action because the situation with the teacher and the book was beginning to annoy me.

One day I waited outside the school for the little dark kid and when he passed by me I jumped him and nailed him to the ground. He immediately asked me in perfect Italian not to hit him and with that gesture of good will we became friends.

That's when I first learned the important principle of "making it" in America, as expressed by that famous American "philosopher", Willie Sutton, who said: "You can get more out of a person with a kind word..... and a gun, than a kind word alone".

In my using the word "Gun" I don't mean violence but I do mean control with a capital "C."

My new Italian friend explained to me what the system was. He explained he did not respond to me in Italian because, if he had, the other kids in the school would have nothing to do with him because they would think he, too, was a DP like me. To be a DP in Canada in the early fifties was comparable to being black in Mississippi before Martin Luther King.

DP by the way, meant Displaced Person, but from my viewpoint, it really should have meant "Delayed Pioneer".

Anyway, he promised to teach me the system and help me with my English.

That's when I decided that I was going to learn everything I could about being like "them." I was going to talk like "them," act like "them" and think like "them." I used to stand in front of a mirror for hours practicing how to say "this" and "that" often spitting because the English sound "th" was foreign to me.

I even began calling myself "Al" instead of "Alex," because "Al" sounded more English than "Alex."

Of course, I had one advantage over the black in Mississippi. Sooner or later, once I got rid of my accent, I could even look like "them."

So from that point on I naively believed that all my problems about identity and prejudice would be over if I looked and acted like "them." Boy, did I have a lot to learn!

Okay, now you may ask, what does all this have to do with Financial Independence.

Well, to begin with, in order to gain any kind of independence or freedom you really have to separate yourself from whatever it is that is keeping you chained up.

Those chains, under the American way of life are (thank God) really self imposed.

If you believe you have to act a certain way so you can please other people into giving you something, you will never be free and will always wind up with less than what you have earned.

You have to be true to yourself and act in the way that your own conscience tells you to act, based on the values that you develop for yourself and not based on values that other people or another culture or society would have imposed on you.

You really have to march to your own drummer! And if that means you will be marching all by yourself, so be it!

What other people think of you should never be an issue when it comes to your decisions or your actions. If something you do would offend others or makes them think less of you, as long as you are acting within your conscience, it shouldn't matter.

Be true to yourself and to hell with the rest of the world!

Then, whatever opportunities happen to present themselves to you, you don't need to wait for other people to give them to you. You just reach out and take them.

I may have been able to learn to talk like "them" and act like "them," and do all the things that "them" do and get invited to their parties and to their clubs, but I could never be "them" because in this Universe, my particular time and space coordinates just didn't call for that position.

So the first step in attaining my independence meant that I had to find out what my personal time and space coordinates were, and go from there.

I wasn't here to please anybody but myself. And I learned that my value to other people was measured not in how I looked or acted or what I said, but simply what I had that other people wanted.

So the more I accumulated of what other people wanted, the more leverage I had to trade for those things I really wanted.

When I learned that, life became a lot simpler and a lot less frustrating.

Prejudice and discrimination were no longer an issue!

Taking the attitude that discrimination and prejudice did not exist in the world that I created for myself, but only existed if I tried to live in other peoples' worlds, was the first step in attaining my independence.

As soon as I became comfortable with "wearing" this attitude, I began feeling good about myself.

The second was the realization that I didn't have to live up to any image of economic status. I didn't have to compete with my neighbors for a snazzier car. And just because I occupied a certain economic position, I didn't have to make my spending patterns commensurate with that position. I became free to spend whatever I wanted to spend, not because my income or my bank account called for it but because I spent what my conscience told me was right for me to spend because that pattern was consistent with the values I had set for myself.

This is not just a difficult point to grasp but also to put into practice. Yet it is critical if you want to avoid the trap that our Mr. Executive or the Duckworths got themselves into.

Once the elements that comprised this attitude became part of my being, I felt a confidence in myself I had never experienced in the past.

The American system of ours, call it Americanism, call it Capitalism,
call it what you like, gives each and every one of us a great
opportunity if we only seize it with both hands and make the most of it.

AL CAPONE, 1929

"Think and Grow Rich":

There is another important factor we need to touch on that is part of this "independence" equation.

That factor is just plain old fashioned thinking.

It seems that the more efficient we become because of technology, the more productive we become and the higher an income we generate as a result. The problem is that because we are so productive, we never have time to think about what we should be doing with all this raw productivity and all this income that is flowing through our hands.

A perfect example of this is what cellular phones have done to our lives.

If you look at the car next to you, chances are the driver has one ear glued to the phone. In restaurants you see people with a fork in one hand and a cellular phone in the other.

People wait for elevators, stroll through the park and hail cabs with a phone pressed to their ear.

Before cellular phones, many of us used those precious moments between meetings, stalled in traffic or walking to the next rendezvous as an opportunity to think and make plans about our lives.

With cellular phones and other technological gadgets, we have become more productive, while spending less time trying to figure out what to do next. We are moving faster while knowing less about where we are headed. We are like the pilot who announces: "We are lost, but we are making good time!"

We have more money going through our hands, yet we are more broke than we have ever been.

W. Clement Stone, a self-made billionaire, whom I once had the pleasure of meeting, co-authored a book called "Think and Grow Rich." It's thesis was simple.

If you contemplate deeply about where you want to be and how you should get there, your instincts will carry you there automatically.

The key is to think yourself into financial independence. Believe me, the concept works like magic.

But we have allowed high-tech toys to soak up all our thinking time.

That has helped us produce ever increasing cash flows, yet we haven't taken the time to figure out how these cash flows could make us rich and financially independent.

The operation was a success but the patient died.

Should we consider then, dumping our cellular phone over the next bridge we come to? I don't own one, but then again, it's your nickel.

If You Hang on to Your Bad Decisions, You Will Spend Your Life Defending Your Own Stupidity Instead of Getting Rich:

Repeatedly in my market operations I have sold a stock while it was rising - and that has been one reason why I have held on to my fortune.

BERNARD BARUCH, 1957

Hanging on to our losses is another factor that contributes to our constant dependence on income.

The classic example is buying a stock for $50 a share, watching it slide to $20 a share, and then holding on to it forever, hoping the price might come back up.

You kid yourself into believing that since you've already made the investment, you may as well hang on until it pays off.

It's amazing how many people buy stock when the price is rising, but refuse to buy more of the same stock once the price has fallen yet still hang on to the original purchase.

If you have enough faith that the stock will go up, then why not buy more? If not, why hang on to the old stock?

Shouldn't you also buy more of the same stock at the lower price so that when it makes a comeback, you will not only get your money back but make a profit?

The reason, I believe, we don't buy more of the same stock or sell what we have at a loss is not because of any conviction about the stock but because we have a deathly fear of admitting our mistakes and cutting our losses.

In other words, we allow our egos to drive our business judgement.

This thinking touches every part of our lives and not just as it may relate to investments.

For example, many people hang on to a bad marriage just because: "I've invested fifteen years of my life in this marriage." But if asked whether they would do it again, the answer most often is an emphatic "No!" Does that make sense?

How about staying in an unpleasant, dead end job because you've "invested ten years with this company?" Or hanging on to a losing business until it drives us into bankruptcy, because it made money once before? Or living in a city even though you hate it because you've "established some roots there?"

The one that really takes the cake is signing up for a weight loss program, an exercise class, self-improvement program, or educational course, only to realize that it's not what you had in mind, yet staying through the program, wasting more time and perhaps money "just because you have already paid for it."

Or just plain sitting through a movie you didn't like "just because you already paid for the ticket."

The analogy here is, "Since I've already wasted some time and money, I may as well waste more time and money."

This is the kind of thinking that keeps most people broke and miserable because they are throwing good money after bad while doing things that they really don't like doing.

Yet most people will regard this "stick-to-it" attitude as being "responsible."

Think of it this way: If the past is any indication of the future, then why tie your future to something that has caused you grief - financial or personal- in the past?

Whatever time or money we spent in the past is irretrievable. The only thing that counts is how you invest your time and money in the future.

So the name of the game is to cut your losses and go on to a new chapter in your life.

Don't waste your energies on living with or avoiding payment for past mistakes. End It! Cut it out! Pay for it and be done with it and go on with enjoying your life!

To recap the original thought, in large part, attaining financial independence really depends on your attitude, your values, your ability to be in control of your ego, and your independence from the opinion of others. The "financial" part is incidental to the process and comes to you as a reward for taking control of your emotions, your ego and your insecurities. It just happens!

A mere madness, to live like a wretch and die rich.

ROBERT BURTON, 1621

It's very well to be thrifty, but don't amass a hoard of regrets.

CHARLES D'ORLEANS, 1465

Without frugality none can be rich and with it very few would be poor.

SAMUEL JOHNSON, 1752

As riches grow, care follows, and a thirst for more and more.

HORACE c. 35 B.C.

CHAPTER 18

Do you know what your financial values are?

THROUGHOUT THIS BOOK, I have been mostly using examples of situations in my personal life and how they have helped me form the attitudes that I needed to come out ahead in the money game.

But those attitudes would not have done me much good until and unless I had a set of values firmly in place that were my personal values and not necessarily those that outside influences happened to have programmed into me.

And those values had to be backed by a certain level of integrity without which I would have merely spent my life as a leaf in a pond, tossed around in whichever direction the winds or the currents may carry me.

In conversations with my friends, work colleagues and clients, I came to a conclusion that most of us really do not understand the true meaning of the word "values" let alone even begin to develop a way of controlling which values would become part of our nature and which we may decide to discard as unsuitable. On the contrary, most of us seem to take on "values" as we go along, deciding at the moment whether something is truly important to us or not.

Let's first define "values." To me values are those things in life that we hold out as important over others. For example, to me it is more valuable to know that I am free from having to earn an income than to drive a Maserati in order to have others think I am someone special. My feeling of financial security is more valuable to me than having my ego fed.

The most important point to recognize is that values are relevant. They really depend on the particular situation we are in and the circumstances surrounding that situation. For example, if I really wanted a Maserati, I could wait until I could drive one and still feel that I have enough capital not to have to earn an income.

On the other hand, no matter how much capital I may have, it may hold no value to me to ever drive a Maserati.

In the first example, a Maserati has less value than financial independence but it still has value.

In the second example, a Maserati has no value whatsoever.

Our first decision then is whether we are sacrificing something in favor of something else, or whether we don't want something, regardless of the circumstance.

Every day we are bombarded with challenges from our co-workers, from our friends, from television commercials, with inviting scenarios that would challenge our value system.

Probably the most bombardment comes from advertising. Through this media, we are made to feel inadequate if we don't smoke, drink, dress in the latest fashions, drive the "right" cars, eat the "right" foods, and live a lifestyle that would have us spend all our money on what the advertisers are selling.

If we have not firmly decided what our values are, we can be easily swayed by these "temptations" and become psychological slaves to the whims of the manufacturers who want to sell us their wares.

On the other hand, if we are solidly in touch with what we really want, it will be difficult to be tempted by what someone else may stroke us for having.

So our first assignment in building a strong set of values is to specifically define what those are to us, keeping in mind the particular situation we may be in.

In making that statement, it may appear that what I am really phrasing is an oxy - moron. How can you define strong values, and then change them based on the circumstances? Isn't this wishy- washy thinking? Not at all!

Let's look at some groups or people with strong religious values.

The Amish in Pennsylvannia have etched their values in granite and pass them on from generation to generation without any compromise regardless of the circumstances. As a result, the world has passed them by. They may be very happy in their particular state, but they may also be missing something.

On the other hand, look at the Mormons in Utah or most Jews throughout the world. Their values are just as strong, yet by adjusting them to the specific circumstances of current society, they can function as the most productive group within this constantly changing world.

Now, I am not saying that the Mormons and the Jews are right and the Amish are wrong. All I am saying is that it is up to you to chose your values, and it is up to you to adjust them to particular circumstances if you so wish. If you chose to stay rigid, it is also up to you. However, if you don't sit down and ask yourself what are your values, you will be seduced by every commercial, and every person who happens to blow in your ear and whisper sweet words about how good you'll feel if you do what they suggest.

In doing research for this chapter, I asked a number of people what was important to them from the viewpoint of personal finances. This question was posed to family income groups from $50,000 per year to over $1 million per year.

Here are the answers:

"To pay off my debts."

"To sell my business at my price."

"To have money left over from my paycheck for savings."

"To be assured of my job until I retire."

"To walk into a mall and buy what I want without worrying about the price or how I will pay for it."

"To hit the lottery and not to have to work anymore."

"To have enough money so that I can do something else that didn't pay as much, that I may enjoy a lot more than what I am doing now, yet maintain the same living standard."

"To leave enough capital for my kids so that they have an edge on life."

"To have enough time and money so that I can travel anywhere I want to."

"To buy a bigger house; car; summer home; boat; aeroplane; etc."

As you can see, the goals expressed in these examples were all over the map. They were diverse, yet they weren't much different than what anybody else might say.

I believe that if I kept asking this question to perhaps one thousand people, the answers, within some variations, would keep coming back the same.

What that tells me is that there is very little difference between any of us as it may relate to personal finances. We all want pretty much the same things.

The only difference is how we set our priorities. And this is where developing a hierarchy of values, or a pecking order, of what is important to us becomes critical.

Most of us will take the approach of getting as much as we can at the first opportunity we have to get it.

The secret to beating the money game, I believe, is not to fall prey to that thinking process.

If you have your priorities of values firmly in place, you will progress from one economic level to the next, each time coming out a little bit ahead of where you were before. If you don't, you will be always playing "catch up" and in the end, you will join the 95 percent of the people who are in the poorhouse.

What I mean by priorities is this: If you insist on a more expensive car or house just because you can afford the payments and because you will feel good about showing them off to your friends, neighbors and co-workers, you are losing the game. If on the other hand, you first accumulate the capital to buy those items -maybe not necessarily exactly when you want them but perhaps a little later- you will, in the end "have your cake and eat it too."

These values are universal.

"Don't put the cart before the horse."

"Success is a cinch by the inch, and hard by the yard."

"Don't try to hit a home run every time you are at bat."

"A penny saved is a penny earned."

"Penny wise and pound foolish."

I could go on and on with age old sayings that reflect these priorities of values but I believe I have made my point. Which is:

There is very little difference between what you want and what most other people want, but if you proceed to get it without first examining what is most important to you, you will probably wind up with very little in the end. You may get to enjoy a few material toys a little sooner, but the price you have to pay for this early use in terms of your health, true happiness and mental well being is much greater than the brief psychic rewards that come with those toys.

My grandmother, who was full of old Russian sayings, hit the nail on the head with one of those sayings.

Translated it means: "The slower you go, the further you'll get."

And not having a firm grasp of your personal values, not someone else's, will put you on a fast track that will place you well behind the starting line at the end of the race.

The flip side of this hunger to overspend, is the inability to let go, and the unreasonable compulsion to hang on for dear life to every nickel.

In some instances, this compulsion may even be worse than being a spend-oholic.

How many of us have read stories of old people dying in poverty, their houses hovels, their clothes rags; eating pet food to save a few pennies, while at the same time, having mattresses, bank accounts and brokerage accounts, stuffed with hundreds of thousands of dollars or perhaps even millions.

This fear to spend which eventually turns into a compulsion, can also be traced to "values."

In this case, having the money becomes more valuable to someone than the things that money is used for. In other words, instead of capital being a vehicle that one uses to reach one's own personal goals, capital becomes a goal in itself for its own sake. Once again, if this "Mr. or Mrs. Miser" would take a close look inside themselves and determine what is it that has real value to them, they may take a totally different viewpoint.

Let me illustrate this point with a similar situation I had with one of my clients.

This client was the typical driven business owner. He was the sole stockholder of his company, in his mid-fifties, and even though he has had this business for more than twenty years, he still had not developed a key person who could take over in the event he wanted to retire. Failing to let go of a business that one started and operated over many years is a common fault of small business owners. In his case, he had to be on top of everything, make all the decisions, and know first hand everything that was going on in the business, and all this even though he had over 40 employees which included management and supervisory people.

Because of this inability to let go and delegate responsibilities, he was unable to develop strong management people.

He kept the weak ones and the strong ones would only last a short period of time.

As a result, he was putting in 12 to 14 hour days, six days a week and rarely took a vacation.

He didn't exercise much and his diet made him overweight. I guess the stress and the overwork finally got to him because before he reached his 57th birthday, he had to go for heart bypass surgery.

After the surgery, his doctor advised him to cut down on his working hours and especially the stress related to his business. The doctor even suggested selling the business.

My client decided to take the doctor's advice, because he had built up a sizeable nest egg through the qualified pension plan he had set up in the business many years earlier, and those funds, combined with his other savings and income properties, when added to the sales price of the business would maintain his spending patterns well beyond his life expectancy.

I came into the case when he wanted input about the value of the business and how the sale might be structured to make it attractive to a potential buyer.

His accountant had done a great job of making a valuation of the business and came up with a figure of $3.2 million.

But when we finally found a buyer, which took a long time because the market for that type of business was not in the highest demand, the offer we got was well below the $3.2 million dollar value.

As a matter of fact, the offer was $850,000 or about one quarter of what we all thought the business was worth.

His accountant advised him to decline the offer and told him that he should not accept a dime below $2.5 million.

The buyer withdrew his offer and there were no other buyers in sight. When he called me that night to tell me his decision, I drove to his house to talk to him. In my heart I knew he had made a mistake. If he could find another buyer, it may take another six months to one year to finally close the deal. By that time, based on his doctor's prognosis, he might be dead.

Here was a clear example of how misguided values can literally be the difference between life and death.

True, the dollar value of the business was much more than the offer. As a matter of fact, the difference was over $2 million. On the other hand, the $850,000 plus his pension plan, plus his other investments would have paid his living expenses for another 30 or 40 years. Way beyond the years he was expected to live.

I got to his house about 10:30 p.m. and the conversation went something like this:

"So you turned down the deal."

"Yes! My accountant told me I would have to be crazy to take $850,000. That's $2 million less than what it's worth. The man insulted me with that chintzy offer!"

"So how much is your life worth?" I said.

He thought about that question and I could immediately see he saw my point. "Thanks," he said.

He called me the next day to tell me he accepted the offer. His accountant won't speak to me anymore because he thinks I gave him bad professional advice. How could anyone in the business of Personal Financial Counseling possibly advise his client to accept a sales price for a business of one quarter of its value?

It's been seven years since this happened. My client is now 64 years old and he calls me now and then.

I feel good about myself. So where is the value?

Jack Benny used to tell a joke about when he was once accosted by two muggers with guns:

"Your money or your life?" they said.

Jack Benny's reply was: "I'm thinking it over."

What is the value of your life?

What is the value of feeling good if you spend money that you can afford on things you will enjoy?

Part of the process of developing your personal values as they may relate to your finances, is to be sure you know what the things you want are worth to you, and which things you are willing to give up in order to gain others.

You have got to know how to be a trader of your own values. And that takes a lot of thought!

Misers are very good people; they amass wealth for those who wish their dealth.

STANISLAUS LESZCYNSKI, 1763

Men are divided between those who are thrifty as if they would live forever, and those who are as extravagant as if they were going to die the next day.

ARISTOTLE, c. 360 B.C.

What is the difference whether you squander all you have, or never use your saving?

HORACE, c. 35 B.C.

Many a man has found the acquisition of wealth only a change, not an end of miseries.

SENECA, c. A.D. 30

The Income Tax has made more liars out of the American people than golf has.

WILL ROGERS, 1924

CHAPTER 19

Summary of the forces that rob you of your capital and how to deal with them

THROUGHOUT THIS BOOK, we have explored different forces that act against us and prevent us from creating capital, and once we have created it, keep us from hanging on to it.

Many times we have seen, heard of, read about or, perhaps, even experienced first hand individuals who one minute appeared to be on top of the world financially, and the next minute were close to personal bankruptcy.

Unfortunately, the system is such that if we are not aware of those forces that act against us and our capital, we will work hard all our lives, live in constant fear of losing our jobs or businesses and, in the end, wind up broke.

Few of us have an opportunity to experience the feeling of being free and independent of earned income.

The only way to reach this state of "financial independence" is by recognizing what consumes our capital, and doing something about it while we still have some energy years left.

As we discussed, some of those forces involve our emotions, our attitudes and our values, and are internal in nature and are controllable by exercising some discipline; others are external and we have no contol over them. However, if we know what they are, we can prepare to minimize their damage.

The attitudinal or internal forces mainly center around our egos, our pride and our greed. They are integrated with our values, our definition of "needs," discipline, and our desire to be accepted by our peers and be part of a "group."

They usually manifest themselves and consume our capital by forcing us to live outside our means. They represent:

Keeping up the image we percieve that may be expected of us.

Trying to make as much money as possible both in earned income and on our investments instead on focusing on what we really need and want out of life.

Reactive overspending by having our purchases dictated not by what we need but by what we think other people may expect from us.

Justifying our worth by working too hard.

Competing with our friends and neighbors for a "higher status" whatever that happens to be. .

Having a compulsive drive to display our "wealth."

Trying to be that which we are not. Not being true to ourselves.

Using our energies negatively by "competing" with our "enemies" and trying to be a "winner."

Hanging on to our capital for no apparent reason and denying ourselves the enjoyment from it.

Wanting something now and paying for it later.

Avoiding payment for our past mistakes and hanging on to our losses.

We have the ultimate control over the above forces and all we need to do is make up our minds that we will no longer respond to them in the same way as we did before, the way that 99.9 percent of the world responds to them. All we have to do is cut our own path and march to our own drummer and not follow the crowd.

On the other hand, we have little or no control over the external forces that rob us of our capital. All we can do is prepare for them and minimize their effect when it happens.

Those forces represent:

Inflation

Taxflation

Business Downturn

Taxes/Government Confiscation

Lawsuit

Financial Markets Volatility

Commissions received by those who advise us in making financial and other investment purchases

Divorce and/or breakup of business partnerships

The biggest handicap is that if we are employed by someone else, we spend most of our productive time improving other people's capital position, while we give very little thought to improving our own.

For some reason, enhancing our capital is always placed on the back burner while we expend our energies for somebody else.

Our focus, instead of being placed on creating capital for ourselves, is wrongly placed on ingratiating ourselves and being more productive for our employers so that we can earn an ever higher income.

We focus on earned income instead of on capital. And that is why we fail.

To be successful in attaining our own financial independence, we have to PAY OURSELVES FIRST with our time, effort and ingenuity. Only those energies that are left over should be "sold to the highest bidder" and given to someone else.

Here are what I call my "COMMANDMENTS OF FINANCIAL SELF DEFENCE":

1. We must spend less than what we earn. We should target our expenses, and then PAY OURSELVES FIRST by making the first bill payment to SAVINGS.

2. Look for opportunities to convert income to capital, and to create new capital. Then hang on to it and not spend it on consumables but let it grow.

3. Only use income to purchase consumables. Never use capital for consumables.

4. Avoid borrowing. Use leverage only for capital purchases and investments, and never for consumables.

5. Don't use "Return on Investment" as a measuring rod for your financial progress. Only use "Wealth Factor" as the measure.

What's the use of getting a high return on investment and taking the risk to capital that goes with it, if you are not paying off enough debt or saving enough from income to offset inflation?

6. Never use earned income as a measure of your "wealth". The only measure that counts is the time frame that you can maintain your present standard of living without earning an income. Don't kid yourself into thinking that you are rich if you are earning a lot of money and have lot's of assets, yet if you lost your income, your spending pattern will wipe out your assets in just a few months or years.

7. Don't put all your eggs in one basket. Diversify your capital. Use asset allocation techniques to accomplish this. Don't look for the

"best place to put your money."

8. Don't chase after high returns. It is tough enough to accumulate capital without having to give it up to bad investment decisions and incompetent investment advisors. Look to preserve your capital and be happy with "just enough" return. Take your risks only where you have your own "man at work" energies working for you like your own business and personally managed Real Estate. Leave the financial investment risks to the suckers.

9. Don't chase after tax deductions and gimmicks. There is no such thing as a free lunch. Nobody is in the 100 percent tax bracket so that for every dollar you spend that is deductable, remember, sixty six cents is your own hard earned money.

10. Invest in yourself and your family first, before you invest in stocks, bonds and real estate. Your personal development, both professional and intellectual, will bring in a lot higher return on investment than any other outside "investment."

11. Live by your own standard of living and not someone else's. Set your own standards that are right for you regardless of what your "position" may call for.

12. Eliminate "should's" and "ought to's" from your way of life. Live by your personal feeling of right and wrong for that moment and not by obligation to either yourself (because you told yourself you might or might not do something) or to others.

13. First loyalty should be to yourself. And if loyalty to an employer or some other party coincides with your best interests, that is fine. If not, your interests must take precedence.

14. Don't be a sheep and follow the crowd. Don't do what other people do. Do that what you feel is right and if it happens to be what everyone is doing, fine. If not, don't be afraid to stand alone.

15. Don't get stuck on past bad investments. Cut your losses and find new approaches. If you made mistakes, don't try to avoid paying for them. Pay the price and get on with your life.

16. Accept new challanges even if they involve risk. Sometimes staying with old habits may represent a greater risk.

17. Pride is a terrible emotion. Do not allow pride to stand in the way of making the right decision. Do that which you feel is right and not necessarily that which will help you "save face."

18. If you must get divorced, don't blame your spouse. Do it before the ugliness starts. Don't follow your lawyer's "advice." Even though he means well because his or her job is to "defend the best

interests of his client", he will place you in an adversary position where you may wind up with more dollars, but you may do irreparable harm to your children and your own mental well-being.

19. Don't look for "enemies" to compete with. Have the courage to find your own arena where there is no competition. Don't strive to be a "winner."

20. As you get older and you reach your level of financial independence, use your capital for your enjoyment. Don't accumulate it strictly for the sake of accumulating capital. After you take care of your family, along with any charitable interests you may have, plan to spend your last nickel with your last breath. Anything that is left over after you die has been a waste of your energies to keep it. Life is too short to ruin it for a little extra money that you or someone else will spend anyway.

21. Believe in the "natural order" of payment. Everything has a price. Be ready to pay that price in advance and if you make a mistake, don't waste your energies in avoiding the payment that is due.

If you follow the above "Commandments of Financial Self Defence," within a reasonably short time, perhaps ten years or less, regardless of your present income, you should reach a point where earned income becomes optional. If you ignore these "commandments" as most people do, you too will wind up broke. Harsh words, but in my experience they are true.

There is a story which comes to mind that deals with the above statement about Confucius and a young man. The young man had a bird in his hands behind his back, and he decided that he was going to play a trick on the wise old prophet. He asked Confucius if the bird was alive or dead. If Confucius said the bird was dead, he would show him the live bird and prove him wrong. If he said the bird was alive, he would crush it with his hands and show him the dead bird. Either way, he felt, the wise prophet would be proven wrong.

When Confucius was finally confronted by the young man and asked the question, his response was: "The bird is in your hands".

And that folks, is where your capital is. It is entirely up to you whether you are going to get to keep it or in the end, if you, too (like most people) will let it slip through your fingers and give it up to the forces that are working to take it away from you.

"YOUR CAPITAL IS IN YOUR HANDS!"

Index

If you enjoyed this book and felt it may have created a positive change in your life, why not share it with some people you care about.

We can send additional copies to you or we can send the book directly to them. Send your orders to: E.B.A., Inc., PUBLISHING DIVISION, #33 Bolivia Street, 4th Floor, Hato Rey, P.R. 00917. Fax (809) 751-1284.

ORDER FORM

Please send _____ copies of $...making it and keeping it! @ $22.95 plus $3.00 for postage and handling for one copy, $43.95 plus $4.00 for postage and handling for 2 copies, $59.95 plus $5.00 for postage and handling for 3 copies. 4 to 10 copies @ $19.00 each plus $1.00 each for postage and handling.

If you would like a 45 minute audio cassette tape that summarizes the essence of $...making it and keeping it! included with each book, add $7.00 for each tape ordered. A $11.95 value if purchased separately.	This book and cassette is available at special quantity discounts when purchased in bulk by corporations, organizations or groups. Special imprints, messages and excerpts can be produced to suit your needs. For more information write to E.B.A. Inc., PUBLISHING DIVISION, #33 Bolivia St., 4th Floor, Hato Rey, P.R. 00917. Fax (809) 751-1284.

[ ] Yes, Please include _____ copies of the audio cassette with my book order @ $7.00 each. ($11.95 if ordering cassette separately)

Total order $_____ [ ] Check   [ ] Money Order
(Payable to E.B.A. Inc.)

[ ] Credit card information: Visa/MasterCard

Credit Card # _____
Exp. Date   _____
Issuing Bank _____
Signature   _____

Your Name   _____
Your Address _____
             _____
             _____

Ship books to: [ ] My address   [ ] Directly to names listed below

Name   _____   Name   _____
Address _____   Address _____
        _____   _____

Name   _____   Name   _____
Address _____   Address _____
        _____   _____

If you would like to receive, (free of charge), a six months subscription to *$...making it and keeping it! REPORT$,* our special personal finance and lifestyle letter designed to keep you on track toward achieving financial well-being and independence, fill out the order form below.

[ ] YES, I want to take charge of my financial future and start living my dreams! Enroll me for a free 6 months subscription to the *$...making it and keeping it! REPORT$.*

Your Name _____

Business or Profession _____

Address_____

_____

Phone #_____

Send to:
E.B.A., INC.
PUBLISHING DIVISION
#33 Bolivia Street, 4th Floor, Hato Rey, P.R. 00917
Fax (809) 751-1284

NOTE: This offer is limited and can be withdrawn or modified at any time without notice.

If you have enjoyed *$...making it and keeping it!,* and would like a 45 minute audio cassette tape in which Alexander Odishelidze summarizes the essence of the key attitudes and values that will help you achieve Financial Independence, please fill out the enclosed order form.

[ ]   YES, please send me _____ copies of the motivational tape by Alexander Odishelidze that summarizes the attitudes and values of *$...making it and keeping it!*

@ $11.95 each plus $1 postage and handling.

Total Order $_____ [ ] Check   [ ] Money Order
(Payable to E.B.A. Inc.)

[ ] Credit card information: Visa/MasterCard

Credit Card #   _____
Exp. Date   _____
Issuing Date   _____
Signature   _____

Name   _____
Address   _____
                _____
                _____

Send to:
E.B.A., INC.
PUBLISHING DIVISION
#33 Bolivia Street, 4th Floor, Hato Rey, P.R. 00917
Fax (809) 751-1284